The Wrong Kind of Son

A Memoir of a Narcissistic Father's Abuse, Survival, and Finding Peace After the Storm.

by **Jeff Peace**

Salty Driftwood Publishing LLC
Saint Augustine, Florida

Copyright

First Edition

ISBN

eBook: 979-8-9936933-0-9
Paperback: 979-8-9936933-1-6

Salty Driftwood Publishing LLC
Saint Augustine, Florida

Dedication

For my mom, who always came when I called, and who loved the right kind of son without conditions.

For my husband and daughter, who remind me what real love feels like every day.

And for anyone who built their peace from someone else's storm.

Before The Story

Memoirs are strange things; we write them with one eye on the past and one eye on the present, hoping the truth will hold steady when both lenses blur. For me, this book was never about proving what happened, but about naming what it felt like. The record of my life doesn't live in court documents or photographs; it lives in the tightness of my chest, the echoes of words that never left my ears, and the relief that finally came when silence meant peace instead of punishment.

Note: This memoir contains descriptions of emotional and psychological abuse, manipulation, and family trauma. If those experiences are part of your story too, please take care while reading.

Epigraph

(Letter to my father, who is still living at the time of this writing.)

Dear Dad,

Maybe you'll read this one day. Maybe you won't. I don't care. But either way, these are the words I need to say; clearly, finally, and without any filter. This isn't a plea, and it's definitely not a conversation. It's the truth as I've come to know it, after years of confusion, silence, and second-guessing myself. I'm writing this for *me*. If you ever do read it, understand: this isn't a request for closure. It's a statement of it.

You built your world on control. On twisting words, rewriting events, and making others doubt themselves so you could stay on top. You were charming when it served you, generous when it looked good, and dismissive the second someone tried to hold you accountable.

You played the role of the successful, enlightened man, claiming to care about fairness, compassion, and decency. But behind closed doors, you manipulated those closest to you. You treated your children as extensions of your ego, not people with feelings, boundaries, or choices. When we resisted, you didn't listen. You doubled down. You made our lives harder until we gave up fighting you.

You created an environment where disagreement was disrespect. Where compliance was the only thing you valued. You forced decisions, dismissed discomfort, and justified every boundary you crossed as "necessary" or "logical." It wasn't logic. It was dominance. And I clearly see that now.

I see how calculated you were.

I see how intentional your actions were. I see how you used people, spun false narratives, and dressed it up as guidance, trying to create a rift. I see how you positioned yourself as the victim when you were actually the architect.

You spent a lifetime needing people to see you as the smartest person in the room. But intelligence without empathy is just cruelty with a vocabulary.

And let me be clear about something else: I couldn't care less what you do with your will or inheritance after you're gone. I've already built my life independently, without needing anything from you, and I'll continue to build it—without your permission, without your approval, and certainly without your validation.

You even tried to force your last name on me in court, back when I was too young to have a voice, as if a name could somehow tether me to your legacy. I'm grateful that judge saw through your manipulation and ruled against it. I have no interest in carrying a name that's bound to a history of control, guilt, and emotional manipulation.

And here's the part that matters: You don't get to control the ending. You don't get the resolution you think you are entitled to or deserve. You don't get understanding. You don't get forgiveness handed to you just because time passed.

You won't get the closure that *you* want—because this time, it's not about you.

This is mine.

This is my line in the sand. This is where I stop carrying what you refused to own. This is where the cycle breaks.

This peace? This clarity? This strength? They belong to me now. And you can't touch them.

— Jeff

Author's Note

This book began as that letter, which I never meant to send.

For years, I carried pieces of my childhood around like evidence: half-remembered scenes, phrases that wouldn't stop echoing, small moments that somehow explained everything and nothing at the same time. Writing them down was the only way to decide what still belonged to me.

The memories in these pages are mine. They are as true as I can make them, shaped by time, distance, and the limits of perspective. I have changed some names and condensed certain events, not to blur the truth, but to protect the people who can't (or won't) speak for themselves.

I didn't write this book to accuse or to forgive. I wrote it to tell the truth of what it felt like to grow up inside a story someone else kept rewriting, and to finally write my own ending.

If you see yourself somewhere in these pages, I hope it's in the moments of survival, not in the harm.

If you've ever had to rebuild your sense of home from the inside out, I hope you find some part of yourself here, too.

With love, always — in every color,
— Jeff Peace

Chapter 1 – The Day I Stopped Being His Son

It was Christmas Eve 2017. My husband, Dan, was pulling warm cinnamon buns and chocolate croissants from the oven when I checked my watch and felt that familiar knot in my stomach; 9:03 a.m., and still no call or text. The light from the kitchen window hit the sugar glaze and made everything look peaceful, domestic, almost cinematic. It could have been a commercial for a happy life, if not for the hollow expectation sitting in my chest.

My father had promised to stop by early to drop off the food he'd made for us as a Christmas gift. He wasn't coming to eat. He'd made that clear, since there wouldn't be enough time. This was a peace offering, an attempt to smooth over whatever jagged thing had been living between us since the wedding. He'd never seen the house we moved into that November, so this visit was meant to be his first glimpse, his chance to pretend everything was fine again.

I told myself I was being nice by agreeing to having him over. One last attempt at civility, a small window for him to show up and prove he could behave. Truthfully, I was already near the edge of cutting him off. The wedding had left bruises that still hadn't faded, and this visit felt like a test I already knew the outcome of.

He loved gestures that looked generous from the outside, the kind that let him look like the bigger person. If you didn't know the history, you'd think it was kind of him to cook. But

I knew better. Every gift from him came wrapped in the expectation of gratitude, like a leash tucked inside a ribbon.

In the past, when things were still good, or maybe just quieter, he would cook some of our favorite dishes and drop them off for Christmas. This time, he'd said, "Everything should be ready for me to meet you in the morning before you have to leave for your plans."

He had a way of making even promises sound like conditions, as if his punctuality were a favor I had to earn.

I wanted to believe him. I really did. Hope is a hard habit to break, especially when it's tied to the idea that maybe this time will be different. Every time he dangled a normal interaction in front of me, some part of me still reached for it.

I should have known when he kept asking which route was best to get here. There were three main ways, and somehow none of them were right for him: one was too far out of the way toward the city, one was a toll road, and the last was too direct and had too many stoplights. Every option, it seemed, was a personal inconvenience. I could hear the irritation in his voice even over the phone, that familiar edge that said the problem was never the directions, it was always me. That's how it had always been; nothing simple stayed simple.

By ten o'clock, the croissants and cinnamon buns were cooling, the kitchen filled with the smell of warmth and hope, two things that would never describe my father. Outside, the sky was that washed-out December gray that never quite turns to daylight. Dan moved easily around me, humming to some holiday playlist, and I tried to match his calm. I wanted the day to stay light, to stay ours. But my body was already listening for tires on the driveway, waiting for the performance to begin.

We were supposed to leave our house by one to see my other family and arrive in time for their festivities. The plan was simple: he'd stop by, hand off the food that he wanted to make, maybe stay a few minutes to see the new house, and we'd wish each other Merry Christmas like normal people.

It sounded so ordinary when I said it out loud, like something every family does. The kind of scene people post on Facebook, with paper plates, laughter, half-eaten cookies, and maybe a family photo before everyone goes their separate ways. I wanted that simplicity so badly it almost felt childish to admit. But underneath it all, I knew that nothing involving my father ever stayed ordinary. There was always a cost, always an invisible test I didn't know I was taking until I failed it.

I kept checking the window anyway. Each glance felt like opening the door to an old wound, knowing exactly what waited on the other side and still looking. The condensation on the glass had started to collect into water drops from the heat inside, thin rivers streaking downward like time itself giving up.

Ten-thirty turned into eleven. My stomach turned with it. The phone stayed silent.

"You think he's coming?" Dan asked.

"He said he would."

Dan raised an eyebrow but didn't answer. He didn't have to. The silence between us said everything. It wasn't judgment. It was the kind of shared understanding that only comes from watching someone you love get disappointed the same way, over and over.

At eleven-fifteen, I finally called. No answer.

At eleven-thirty, I tried again. He picked up this time, his voice light and airy, with the tone that always meant you're already losing this conversation.

"I'm still cooking," he said. "Running a little behind. You're still home, right?"

"We have to leave soon," I said. "By one, or we'll be late."

"I'm heading out soon, so you'll still make it," he replied, and hung up before I could respond.

That was his way: get in, deliver the line, and hang up before reality had a chance to argue. Conversations with him were like trying to hold water in your hands; by the time you realized what was happening, it was gone, and somehow the emptiness felt like your fault.

I tried to stay positive. I wanted to believe him. I told myself he was probably plating the food, finding containers, maybe packing up the car. Anything to quiet the noise in my chest that said he wasn't coming.

Noon came and went. Still no sign of him.

At 12:30, I called again.

He answered, his voice suddenly heavy with exaggerated disappointment. I told him we couldn't wait any longer, especially since he still hadn't even left his house and we were at least 30 minutes from him.

"Well," he said, smooth as oil over ice, "I suppose all this food I spent hours cooking for you will just end up in the trash. What a waste."

There it was. The old guilt, smooth and familiar as a blade.

He didn't yell. He didn't even sound upset. He said it in that tone that made me feel like the selfish one for daring to have plans that didn't include him, for refusing to orbit around his lateness. It was the same tone that used to make me apologize before I even knew what I'd done wrong. The same tone that could turn generosity into leverage in five words or less.

Something inside me hardened. My hand curled into a fist before I realized it. The air felt thick, my pulse loud in my ears. For the first time, I didn't feel small. I felt something sharper. I could almost feel bull horns pushing through my temples: anger, defiance, the first spark of something unrecognizable but strong. Maybe it was every Christmas that had ended in silence. Maybe it was every phone call that turned into an interrogation. Maybe it was the memory of him at our wedding the year before, spreading rumors to our guests that my husband's family had paid for everything, telling people it was their celebration, not mine. Maybe it was the way he'd once asked who "the girl" was in my marriage.

Whatever it was, I was done.

"You know what?" I said, my voice shaking but certain. "We'll come pick it up. We'll be there in thirty minutes, plus it's on the way to where we're going anyway. That way, the food doesn't have go to waste."

Silence stretched on the line. I could almost hear his brain trying to calculate what I just said, trying to make sense of a son who suddenly wasn't following the script.

"You'll what?" he asked finally.

"We'll come get it. Half an hour."

Another pause. Then, cold and flat as a closing door: "Okay. See you then."

When the call ended, I stood there for a moment staring at the phone, half expecting it to ring again. It didn't. The silence that followed wasn't relief exactly. It was something better. Control, maybe. The smallest proof that I could still choose how this day would go.

We quickly loaded into the SUV with that silence still ringing between us. It wasn't angry silence; it was the kind that hummed just beneath the surface, the kind that carries the weight of everything not said. The car doors closed, and it felt like sealing ourselves into a capsule of obligation. Outside, the sky had turned the color of old pewter, the kind of winter light that flattens everything it touches. The road to his house wound through bare trees and half-frozen fields. The branches were skeletal against the gray, bending slightly in the wind, as if even the trees were bracing for what waited ahead.

I hadn't seen him in almost a year. I told myself I wasn't nervous, but my chest knew better. It pulsed tight, that strange blend of dread and duty that I'd been trained to call love. I kept thinking of all the times I'd made this drive before, with each visit a fresh hope that maybe this time would be normal, each return trip a quiet promise to myself that it would be the last.

Dan drove. I watched the scenery slide past, familiar and foreign at the same time. Every mile felt like years collapsing inward, the drive to a childhood home that never felt like one. The hum of the tires became a kind of metronome for my heartbeat, steady and unrelenting. I traced a finger along the window glass, following the condensation trails, pretending to be absorbed in the view while fighting the thought that I was heading back into something I'd spent my whole adult life escaping.

"I don't know why I'm doing this," I said quietly.

"He's your father," Dan said. "I get it."

He meant it kindly, but I felt the sting of it anyway. The word father still carried a weight it hadn't earned. It sounded too gentle for what he was.

I wanted to believe that, too. That some small part of me was just doing the right thing, not repeating the same old pattern. But I knew better. It wasn't duty driving me, it was the muscle memory of guilt.

I felt like a kid again and could feel my anxiety level rising, almost to the house, almost to the battlefield of my childhood. Almost to the mess. Almost to the man who made it a warzone. Almost to my father. I caught myself holding my breath, the same way I used to before walking into his house as a teenager, trying to guess which version of him I'd find waiting on the other side of the door.

His driveway looked the same as ever. Ruts from the rain, weeds brushing against both sides of the SUV, that long uphill stretch that always felt like punishment. Cars bottomed out here and usually got stuck in the gravel. Then came the corner near the trees, then the final hill before the last corner, and then finally the house, crouched against the gray sky, siding faded, junk scattered across the yard, a rusted wind chime clanging in the cold breeze. The wooden garage doors were pockmarked with holes where squirrels and cats had clawed through for warmth and refuge from the harsh winter nights.

It wasn't neglect exactly; it was ego rot. The kind that seeps into every surface of a place until it mirrors its owner. Even the air here smelled different: damp, metallic, old. I could feel the past rising from the ground like steam.

When we parked, I sat for a moment, staring at the front door. The engine and exhaust ticked as it cooled, a slow, hollow sound that filled the silence between us. I could taste the metallic dryness of my mouth, the way it always happened before seeing him, as if my body remembered something my mind was trying to forget. Through the kitchen window, I could see the light glowing yellow, too bright against the gray afternoon. It was the same window where, decades earlier, he'd watched me through the glass as I read the Bible aloud on Sunday mornings on the porch bench. Even then, I knew he wasn't listening for the words, he was watching for mistakes. For control. For proof that I still feared him.

"Let's get this over with," I said, my voice flat.

We got out of the car and started up the walkway. The slate tiles smooth under our shoes. The cold hit hard with that thin winter air that stung my lungs and smelled faintly of damp earth and fireplace. He was already on the porch, waiting. He greeted us each with a handshake, a small smile, too practiced, as if he were already rewriting the story for whoever he'd tell it to later. That smile was his mask, and I knew it. I'd seen it in courtrooms, at family gatherings, in every photo where he played the doting father. The performance had always been for everyone else.

When we stepped inside, the door creaked closed behind us, and the sound of it sent chills straight through me. That sound matched a memory of wood and metal groaning. Might as well have been the house whispering: Welcome back to hell.

The air changed instantly, heavier, almost damp with history. I could feel my shoulders tense without realizing it, my pulse quicken, my body falling into its old defensive posture, as if bracing for impact.

The kitchen lights were harsh, bouncing off cluttered counters and stacks of unopened mail. The air smelled of food and old paper. The mix was nauseating: sweet, stale, and strangely familiar. Like time had rotted here but no one had noticed. He stood behind the island, carving something with a dull knife while the TV blared sports from the next room. The volume was too loud, almost intentionally so—his way of filling silence before anyone could say something real.

The same island where he'd once spread open that newspaper years ago, the one announcing Hawaii's legalization of gay marriage, and told me, in front of everyone, that I could "always go there." He'd watched me read it, waiting for the humiliation to land. He'd smiled then too, not out of joy but satisfaction, the kind that comes from drawing blood without lifting a hand. Even now, decades later, I could feel the heat of all those eyes on me, the confusion, the shame. The humiliation had been public, but the aftermath of my silence, and my shrinking; that had been private. The same counter. The same man. The same calculated cruelty disguised as casual conversation.

I told him I needed to use the bathroom and started down the hall toward the powder room.

"That one's broken!" he called after me—right as I stepped inside and saw it for myself.

The toilet sat cracked, the tank lid off, the water line shut tight. Only one lightbulb worked on the fixture above the mirror that normally had five. Dust and grime clung to the porcelain like it had been holding its breath for years. A half-used roll of paper sat on the counter, curled in on itself, yellowing at the edges. Even the mirror had gone cloudy, like it was tired of reflecting this place. Of course it was broken. Everything in this house eventually broke: pipes, ceilings, people. His voice echoed faintly down the hallway, muffled by the walls, that same defensive tone he used when caught off guard. It wasn't embarrassment; it was control slipping, and he hated that.

I climbed the stairs to the guest bathroom instead. The air hit me first—stale, thick with that sour dampness that lives where light doesn't reach. Each step groaned under my weight, a deep wooden sigh that made it sound like the house itself didn't want me there. The hallway smelled faintly of mildew and old paint, that scent that always makes you think of things left undone.

The tub was filled with boxes, swollen and soft from humidity, stacked like they'd been forgotten mid-move. The toilet was ringed in grime, the floor mottled with yellow stains, the bowl murky under a scum of mildew. The sink, when I glanced at it, looked like it hadn't been touched in years. Just a thin layer of dust collecting the ghosts of every breath ever held in this house. A dead spider sat in the corner of the vanity, curled and brittle. Even stillness had a way of decaying here.

It wasn't just neglect. It was something worse. Like decay had become the language of this place. Every surface told a story of someone who'd stopped caring but refused to let go. The rot wasn't accidental; it was curated. A slow defiance against time itself, the same kind of stubbornness he carried in his bones. Standing there, I realized the house hadn't changed at all; it had simply kept rotting in the same direction it always had. The wallpaper peeled in long vertical strips, like the years themselves were shedding.

It felt like stepping into a mausoleum, a monument to everything that had quietly died here long before this day. The air carried the heaviness of grief, not mine exactly, but something inherited; an accumulation of years spent pretending everything was fine. I'd been in that bathroom so many times as a kid, but I'd never really seen it. Not the slow collapse, not the quiet rot that had been waiting beneath the surface all along. Maybe I couldn't see it then because I was part of it. You don't notice the walls rotting when you're busy holding them up.

Back downstairs, the great room sagged under the same weight of decay. It wasn't just the furniture, it was the air itself, thick with dust and resignation. The couch was shoved against the wall, two folding tables crowded with potted plants huddled in the middle like survivors after a storm. The plants were leggy and pale, reaching sideways toward a light that never really found them, much like everything else that lived here. The tile floor was stained in paths that showed exactly where he still walked and where he hadn't bothered in years.

When I looked up, I saw the sky through a large hole in the ceiling; dark, soft-edged, surrounded by mildew that spidered across the drywall ceiling. It looked alive, like veins spreading from a wound. The cold air slipped through it in drafts that carried the smell of wet wood and rot. I could hear the faint drip of water somewhere, steady and patient, as if even the house was counting time differently here.

He laughed when he noticed me staring. "That's where the plants get watered when it rains," he said.

His tone was light, almost proud, like a man giving a house tour instead of explaining a gaping wound in his roof. I couldn't tell if it was denial or theater anymore—maybe both. He'd always preferred humor to accountability. To him, a broken ceiling wasn't a problem, it was an anecdote.

The roof had leaked for as long as I could remember after the rebuild, and was now a king-bed-sized hole in the ceiling. The fire in 1998 took the first version of this house, but somehow, nineteen years later, it still looked half-burned. The ash was gone, but the energy wasn't. Even the rebuilt walls seemed to sag under the memory of flame, as if the house had never forgiven him for surviving it. I wondered, not for the first time, if he rebuilt it to prove something—to show that nothing, not even fire, could undo him. But the truth was right there above us: it already had.

My father crossed the room toward the wooden double doors leading into the formal dining room. He rapped on them twice, sharp and deliberate. The sound cracked through the room like a command. He didn't knock to ask; he knocked to summon.

A muffled voice came from the other side. My uncle. "What?"

My father knocked again, louder this time. "Ray," he called, his tone oddly urgent, a strange edge of performance in it; half command, half concern, as if even the knock had to remind everyone who was in charge. The pause that followed was thick enough to touch. I could hear the friction between them through the wood, two men whose lives had long ago hardened into hierarchy.

I felt guilty at how my father was coercing my uncle out of the room. It was the kind of guilt I'd carried my whole life. The secondhand kind, the kind that doesn't belong to you but still sticks. Watching him work people like levers always made my stomach twist. Once Uncle Ray opened the door, my father quickly walked through the kitchen and out of the other entrance towards the hallway that leads to the front door. Even now, his exits were always about control, leaving before anyone could decide to follow, always writing the final line of the scene. I realized that was his art form: not conversation, not connection. Just direction.

Uncle Ray appeared a moment later, pushing open the dining room doors. When he saw me and Dan, his whole face changed. He lit up like he'd just seen a ghost he was happy about.

"Hey, how the heck are you, buddy?" he said, his voice softer than I remembered, worn at the edges but still wrapped in that same old warmth. His grin stretched wide, and for a moment, it felt like no time had passed at all. The sound of his voice broke through the air like sunlight in a shuttered room. I hadn't realized how tight my chest had been until that moment. For the first time since walking in, I breathed without effort.

He stayed on the far side of the kitchen island, a cautious distance I understood. The distance wasn't rejection, it was self-preservation. Everyone in this house learned how to gauge safety by the number of steps between themselves and him. He had his own demons, reasons he couldn't live alone anymore, but in that moment, he looked purely happy to see me.

He asked about my job, my life, my family. I introduced him to Dan, and Uncle Ray's grin somehow got bigger. His eyes lit up with the kind of easy acceptance that didn't need to be performed or explained. He asked Dan polite questions, cracked a small joke, and for five minutes, I remembered what family was supposed to feel like: uncomplicated, safe, human. For those few minutes, the house felt almost normal. His laughter filled the kitchen in a way that made me remember what warmth used to sound like here.

Then, from the corner of my eye, I caught a movement near the hallway. My father.

He was half-hidden in the shadow beyond the kitchen light, his head bowed, pretending to busy himself but really just listening. The light fell just short of his face, catching the line of his jaw but not his eyes, and somehow that made it worse.

He looked like part of the wall, something built to watch and never rest. I knew that posture. The stillness wasn't calm. It was calculation. He was absorbing every word between me and Uncle Ray, storing it like ammunition. That was always his gift: to turn affection into data, kindness into leverage.

A cold wave went through me. I could almost feel the energy shift in the room, the way warmth retreats when a predator enters the frame. I knew what would come later and how he'd corner Uncle Ray after I left, how questions would turn to corrections, and corrections would turn to shame. I tried to steer the conversation toward polite goodbyes, knowing this would cost Uncle Ray later.

When we wrapped up, I told him how good it was to see him after all these years. He said the same, wished us well, and turned back toward the dining room where he lived now. His world was contained to a couch, a chair, and a small TV glowing in the dark. I watched the door close behind him, that thin click echoing louder than it should have. In a different family, that would've been the sound of rest. Here, it was the sound of survival.

My father came back into the kitchen after the dining room doors shut behind Ray. The echo of that soft click lingered, a sound too final for such an ordinary door. He stood there a moment, still in the threshold, like he needed to reclaim the air that had just belonged to someone else.

He gave a small, almost wounded laugh. "He never talks to me anymore," he said, shaking his head. "It's like he's mad at me or something. I haven't heard his voice in weeks."

His tone was half-injury, half-performance; the familiar mixture that always asked for pity while daring you to question the story. He spoke like the victim, but the smile pulling at his mouth gave him away. It wasn't pain; it was control disguised as confusion.

He sounded genuinely surprised, even a little offended, that Ray had spoken so easily with me. "I can't believe he talked that long and sounded happy talking to you," he said, as if warmth were something his brother should have withheld out of loyalty. He said it with the same disbelief someone might reserve for betrayal, as if joy were treason. That was the world he built, where affection had sides, and even laughter had to choose allegiance.

Uncle Ray had always been my favorite. When I was young, before I knew the full web of family secrets, I used to wish he'd been my father instead. Uncle Ray was the kind of man who listened with his whole face, who could turn even a simple "how are you" into something that sounded like a prayer. Standing there in that ruined kitchen, I felt that wish surface again, childlike, stupid, and still true.

Dad started boxing up the food, sliding containers into plastic bags so they wouldn't leak. His movements were brisk, practiced, almost militaristic. He wasn't just packing food; he was packing narrative. Every sealed lid, every knotted bag was another prop in his story of generosity.

"I'll walk you out," he said. "I want to help load the car. I want to see what you're driving these days."

Outside, the air was sharp and gray. It bit at my nose and cheeks, cutting through the smell of damp leaves and wood smoke. The cold felt clean—like stepping out of something rotten and remembering how air was supposed to taste. He followed us down the walkway that I remember being so slippery after any rain, bags in hand. He knocked once more on the dining room window, calling for Ray to come look at the car.

"You've gotta see this," he said, his voice too loud, too eager, too manipulative. It wasn't about the car; it was about keeping the spotlight, about making sure no one else held the final moment. Every word he said carried the weight of performance, as if he were narrating his own myth while the credits rolled.

From inside came Ray's muffled reply: "I'll wave from the window."

Through the glass, I saw his hand lift, a small silhouette framed by the dim light of the dining room, the same room he lived in now, surrounded by a couch, a chair, and old memories. The motion was faint, almost trembling, but it said everything: distance, apology, survival. That wave felt like the end of something, though I didn't know what yet.

We loaded the bags into the back of the SUV. My father stood there awkwardly for a moment before extending his hand. It was the same handshake I'd seen him give to strangers—firm, rehearsed, meant to establish dominance rather than affection. The contact felt more like a business transaction than a goodbye. We shook, formal as strangers. Then Dan and I got in.

I pressed the ignition, and the engine came alive with a deep growl. Out of instinct—or maybe defiance—I hit the button that opened the exhaust valves right when it started. The sound roared through the driveway; I could hear it bouncing off the front of the house. The vibration ran through the seat and into my spine, a physical reminder that this was my machine, my noise, my life now. My father flinched slightly, his eyebrows rising, his mouth twitching toward a smile that didn't quite make it. For the first time that day, I didn't flinch back.

We rolled down the gravel hill and back to the main road, leaving the sagging house shrinking in the rearview mirror. The tires slipped slightly on the loose stone, crunching in uneven rhythm, and for a second, I imagined the whole structure collapsing behind us; a rotting house finally giving in. The road curved away, and with every turn the air felt lighter, as if distance itself were medicine. My chest loosened one notch at a time. The smell of mold and old mail gave way to cold winter air that bit at my nose and cleared my head. It felt like breathing for the first time all day.

As his road disappeared behind us, I could still feel it in my body: the pressure in my chest, the small tremor in my hands, the buzzing under my skin that always came after being near him. Driving up to that place earlier, I'd felt it start: the slow tightening, the quiet dread, the old reflexes waking up like soldiers hearing the first siren of a war they thought was over. The sound of the front door closing had pulled me straight back to childhood, to weekends that were supposed to feel like love but felt more like surviving war. I shouldn't still have that reaction. Not as an adult. Not after all this time. But that's the thing about manipulation—it rewires you so completely that even silence starts to sound like command. And he was still doing it, even now, testing the edges of what he could pull. We'd tried to see if a few minutes together could feel normal again, but it didn't. It never would.

I'd thought about cutting him off before, but this was different. I was finally ready. I was sick of that feeling: the anxiety, the shrinking, the carefulness, the way his voice could still rearrange the air in a room. I was sick of living on his terms. I was done mistaking his control for connection. Because once you've survived what I did as his child, there's no version of adulthood where that man deserves another chance.

And as the miles stretched behind us, something in me began to lift; the first breath of real freedom. It hit me then: the dream I'd had since childhood was finally coming true. I would never have to go back to that house again.

Ahead waited the only kind of family on my dad's side that still felt like home; Aunt Cathy, Ellen, Sophie, and Nora. They were Uncle Ray's ex-wife and daughters, the ones who, in their own quiet ways, had escaped too and had to cut him and the rest of the family off. Each of them had built their own little orbit outside of the family's gravitational pull. It wasn't rebellion. It was survival disguised as sanity. None of them kept ties to my father or the rest of his siblings anymore, nor did they keep in contact with Uncle Ray. Like me, they'd stepped away from the chaos and found peace in distance. There was something sacred about that. About survivors finding one another, even if we never called it that out loud.

It felt almost poetic to be heading to spend time with them on Christmas Eve. After the storm I'd just left, it was like driving toward light. When I was a kid, their house was the center of the holiday universe. Every year, the same ritual: carols that turned into competitions, determining who could sing the loudest, and who could make the others laugh mid-verse. The soda bar in the garage where we'd decorate red Solo cups with markers, pour whatever soda we wanted, and top it with cherries or splashes of fruit juice like little mad scientists. Ham dinners with sandwich rolls stacked high, ping pong tournaments in the basement, and computer games glowing in the next room. Every inch of that house had held laughter; even the walls seemed to hum with it.

We were all blissfully ignorant back then; kids spinning in the glow of Christmas lights, unaware of the fractures running through the adults around us. For one night every year, the world felt simple. The grown-ups' smiles looked genuine, the arguments paused, and the air buzzed with that rare magic of being too young to notice dysfunction. The smell of baked ham, the faint sting of pine sap on our fingers, the way the cold hit our faces when we ran outside and came back in pink-cheeked. It was all the proof we needed that good existed.

We didn't know what was brewing in that family, or what storms waited beyond those walls. We just sang, laughed, and believed in something good. And it was good, until it wasn't.

And as we drove through the winter dark now, I realized that belief hadn't died; it had just changed shape. It wasn't about Santa or songs anymore. It was about survival, and about knowing that sometimes peace doesn't come from the people who raised you. It comes from the ones who finally understand why you had to leave.

When we finally reached Aunt Cathy's new house, the world shifted. Her porch light glowed through the afternoon gray like warmth itself. She opened the door before we even knocked, hugging us before we even stepped inside. Sophie and Nora were there, music playing softly in the background, the smell of cinnamon and ham filling the air. Ellen was on Facetime as she lived across the country. It felt safe and familiar in a way that hurt.

I told them about seeing Uncle Ray in an unexpected visit to my dad's house, about how happy he'd been to see me, how he'd asked about my life and my job, and how alive and "with it" he'd seemed in that moment. Aunt Cathy's hand flew to her mouth. Her eyes filled instantly.

"He talked to you?" she said. "Oh, my word."

She sat down hard in a kitchen chair, laughing and crying all at once. "That's the best Christmas gift I could've gotten," she said, wiping her eyes. "He always loved you. You were always special to him, even when things got bad."

Sophie reached for her mother's shoulder. They all nodded, smiling through tears. The room was full of that strange mix of joy and loss; the kind that only exists when love still lives somewhere it isn't safe to touch.

Christmas Eve was the anniversary of the day they met. Aunt Cathy said that every year she still put out the same small decorations they both loved, even though he couldn't be there anymore. "I still love him," she said softly, "and I wish things were different. But we can't safely be near him. Not the way he is now."

Her words hung in the air like a prayer that would never be answered. I nodded, because I understood exactly what she meant. Loving someone doesn't always mean you can stay. Sometimes it just means you carry the memory of who they were before the damage took over.

That night, surrounded by laughter and warmth, I felt something inside me finally unclench. The sound of my cousins' voices, the hum of easy conversation, even the clink of glasses—it all felt like music from a life I'd been locked out of for years. After the tension earlier, I wasn't waiting for a call, or an apology, or a miracle. My phone stayed face down on the counter, and for once I didn't check it. I didn't scan the room for a shadow, didn't brace for a tone shift, didn't measure my words against someone else's reaction.

I wasn't just leaving my father's house. I was leaving the version of myself that still believed he might come back different. It was a quiet kind of freedom, not the cinematic kind with fireworks or closure, but the real kind; the kind that happens when your body realizes the danger has passed, even if your mind hasn't caught up yet. The kind where peace doesn't announce itself; it just arrives, sits beside you, and lets you breathe.

And as the night went on, I realized something both beautiful and brutal: the choice I'd made in that car, driving away from his house for the last time, had begun to feel like peace.

What I didn't realize in that moment was how long the residue of that house would linger. Leaving physically is one thing—leaving emotionally is another battle altogether. Every mile put distance between us, but distance doesn't erase training. My body still scanned for danger, still braced for the sound of his voice. That was the beginning of the long undoing: learning to trust calm again, learning that a quiet day could actually just be quiet.

Even now, as an adult who has built a good life and learned to stand on his own, something about him could still reduce me to that frightened kid. One man shouldn't hold that kind of power in anyone's head, certainly not after decades, and certainly not after everything he did to me. That's what finally pushed me to end it. I was tired of feeling small in rooms I'd outgrown, tired of letting the ghost of his authority live rent-free in my mind. Cutting him off wasn't just a boundary—it was an exorcism.

I didn't know then that peace would last almost a decade, and counting.

I also didn't know that peace would become the mirror that showed me everything I'd spent years trying not to see: the guilt-trips, the manipulation, the quiet kind of control and cruelty that turns a childhood into a warzone.

But peace doesn't just reveal pain. It gives you the strength to face it. For the first time, I could look back without collapsing under the weight of it. The memories that used to feel like live wires had begun to quiet; I could hold them now, study them, name them for what they were. That's what healing really is. Not pretending the past was different, but finally being strong enough to stop flinching when it comes near. Peace didn't erase what happened. It gave me the light to see it clearly.

Chapter 2 – First Bite

My first clear memory of my father isn't a hug or a bedtime story. It's chicken.

Dry, stringy, bland chicken chunks, cut small. I was in a high chair in his kitchen in the old house, old enough for a booster seat at the table, and also old enough to know I didn't want another bite. He stood over me with his hand, fingers slick with grease, trying to push the meat into my mouth, holding the back of my head so I would stop moving away.

I remember thinking, maybe if I bite him, he'll stop. Maybe that's what it takes since asking and crying wasn't working.

So I did. I clamped down, harder than I'd ever bitten anything in my life. He shouted, jerking back, but couldn't free his finger until I let go. The sound of his scream still lives somewhere behind my eyes. I don't know if I drew blood, but I remember the shock on his face, the disbelief that something so small could defy him. His voice broke into a higher pitch than I'd ever heard.

"Laura!" he yelled, his voice cracking. "He bit me! He actually bit me!"

It wasn't so much the pain. It was disbelief that a child so small had fought back. That was my father and me, before I even had words for it: him forcing, me resisting. A lifelong script written before I could read.

Back then, my visitation weekends were spent in that old Craftsman house from 1913, the one with the formal tiled entryway and the glass front door no one used unless they were pretending to have class or guests. It was the kind of door that looked like it belonged to a nicer family, the kind people photographed for real estate flyers to make a place look more respectable than it felt. When my mother brought me there for Halloween to trick or treat, we had to knock on that door like outsiders. She stood behind me, polite smile plastered on, holding my hand. He opened it with that fake charm he used like a weapon, his grin a little too wide, his voice a little too sweet.

Inside, it smelled like furniture polish and old wood; the kind of clean that never feels fresh. Every surface gleamed but somehow looked tired, like the house itself knew it was performing. Even as a kid, I could sense the performance: the fake laugh, the forced warmth, the way he wanted us to see him as something he wasn't.

It was the house he shared with Laura, the woman after my mom, who I lived with during visitation and still love to this day, and with whom I still keep in touch. Laura was the quiet in his storm, the one who taught me small kindnesses he never could.

My brother and sister were born during those years in the Craftsman house, long before he moved on to the next chapter of his performance. I remember their bed and crib set in the bedrooms on the left side of the house with the doors into each room from the hallway and from room to room. Laura treated me as one of her own, even when he made sure I never forgot whose bloodline was whose. She gave warmth where he gave orders, and for a while, the noise of a growing family almost covered the tension that lived in the walls.

My mother never married my father. She saw through the performance fast enough. Just a few months was all it took to realize what he really was. She walked before he could infect her life any further.

But for me, there was no walking away. Just trading one version of his life for another. After Laura came Theresa and her three kids. Then my half-sister, Anna, was born in the new house; a bright, curious baby who would one day learn to live inside the same maze of moods and rules I'd already mapped. The new house he built in 1988 eventually filled up with nine people and a kind of noise that never sounded like home. Laughter that always felt like it was happening for someone else.

And then, in 1998, it all burned down.

Even after the fire, the lessons he taught us about silence and obedience survived intact.

I watched it burn after school, a breaking-news interruption on the TV all the way at my mom's house. Live footage from a news chopper, the smoke curling into a sky that didn't care. My father called me during the news footage to tell me that everyone was out and safe, and then had to run to leave work and get to the house. The news announcer's voice called it "a luxurious home engulfed in flames," but all I saw was a place I never used to walk barefoot in. And I wondered if the announcer saw the inside, would he still say that same line? The video footage was strangely beautiful; orange against gray, flames licking the roofline I knew too well. I remember wondering if the fire would finally erase the smell of that house for good.

My father met all of his women the same way: women unraveling their existing marriages, sitting across from him in his office, asking for legal help. Back then, he specialized in divorce, which made his world a revolving door of people at their weakest, looking for someone to believe them, to save them. He was their attorney first, then their savior, and eventually their undoing. He didn't just win cases; he collected women who mistook his confidence for safety. Each of them started out thinking they'd be the one to fix him, the one who could tame the man who knew how to sound like rescue.

By the time I was eight years old, we were living in the new house he'd built with Laura, his second act, the showpiece of his supposed success, just before their divorce. It was a bigger, luxurious house, but it never felt warmer after Laura moved out. Laura had left behind rooms that still held her décor items, her framed photos, the evidence of what a real home had almost been. Within months, Theresa and her three kids moved in, as if the ink on the last marriage hadn't even dried. The furniture shifted, the photos changed, but the chaos increased.

Together with my father's hoarding, the house got trashed. He filled the garage, basement, closets, and spare rooms with boxes of stuff, broken appliances, half-finished projects, and things he swore he'd fix "someday." The rest of us learned to navigate around the piles like it was normal. The smell of dust and grime became the background noise of those years, a permanent haze that no number of open windows could clear. What had started as a symbol of his success slowly turned into a monument to everything he couldn't let go of.

I used to beg my mom to find some way, anyway, to keep me from going to his house for visitation. I'd start the week before it was time, asking if there was something she could file, some form she could sign, some loophole we hadn't tried yet. I remember sitting at our kitchen table while she packed my small bag, my voice small but relentless: "Please, Mom, don't make me go this time." She'd close the zipper carefully, and tell me she wished she could, but he always wins in court.

She had so little power. As a single mother with extremely limited funds, she knew she couldn't win against a defense attorney who made a living out of twisting rules. He was louder, richer, and legally bulletproof. Her love was real, but it didn't count in court. I even pleaded with her, promising that I'd take the stand myself and tell the judge I didn't want to go and that they'd have to listen, since I was the kid. I imagined the scene, standing there with my small hands gripping the desk on the stand, telling the truth like it would finally matter.

But we both knew how this worked. His manipulation always won. Even when the truth was obvious, it bent itself to him like everyone else did. He never lost.

Until now.

Back then, I thought "winning" would mean not having to see him anymore. Staying at my mom's house full time like my friends, hopefully testifying in court and escaping his hold for good. Sometimes I dreamed he wasn't even my father, that maybe my uncle was instead. To a kid who walked into a warzone every other weekend, those fantasies felt like freedom.

But that doesn't come close to what winning feels like now. Winning as an adult means being free to cut him out completely. It means no more pretending, no more explaining, no more anxiety from his words or his presence. It means knowing I won't be at his funeral, because I already mourned the loss of the father I should have had.

Memory has a way of looping back to the beginning, to the moments that taught you what fear felt like. For me, that beginning always starts the same way: a loud house, the sound of a kettle, and the weight of being watched.

Sunday mornings at his house always smelled like hot tea and control.

That was the environment where Sunday reading began for my sister Julia and me. It wasn't the kind of reading that grows curiosity or love of stories; it was the forced kind that measured obedience.

He called it reading time. We had to sit on the couch in the two-story sunken family room after breakfast, each with a book chosen by him, and read aloud, with everyone else in the house listening, watching. My sister was assigned the children's Bible—always the same one when I was there, its cover worn to gray at the corners. I started with that too, but when I pretended to finish it by flipping two or three pages together over the weekends, he said I could pick something "more grown-up." A magazine, a mystery, a book from the shelf behind the TV. It sounded like freedom, but it wasn't. It just meant he could say I had no excuse.

He stood in the kitchen while we read out loud in the family room, me first, and then Julia. If you stopped, he'd ask why.

If you sighed, he'd ask louder. The rule wasn't eyes on him this time; it was obedience. Don't interrupt. Don't complain. Don't move. Just keep reading aloud.

My sister's voice was small and defeated. She would stumble on a few words, and he'd correct her without looking up. She never got to switch to anything else. It seemed that she was supposed to stay with the children's Bible forever, as if growing up was something she hadn't earned. She read that thing with tears in her eyes every other weekend and I don't recall her ever being able to move on to the next book.

And if I read too quickly, he'd snap—too fast!—and then start quizzing me about what I'd just read. When I couldn't answer, when the words hadn't even had time to sink in, he'd make me start over from the top of the page. So I learned to read just slow enough not to get in trouble, dragging my eyes along the lines until the meaning fell apart. Sometimes I'd have to reread the same paragraph two or three times before he was satisfied.

I used to stare at the clock instead of the page, counting the seconds until I could close the book. The minute hand crawled; the stories blurred. None of it felt holy or like it was helping. It felt like being held underwater and told to breathe slower. Afterward, he'd ask what we learned. My mind went blank. I always said something safe like patience, honesty, kindness. He'd nod like a teacher grading a paper. Then the day would continue, and the house would fill with the sound of him moving through it, the sound of us staying small.

For years that was reading: obligation dressed as virtue. Words became chores, sentences turned into fences. By middle school, whenever anyone asked if I liked to read, I said no before they even finished the question. I said it like a warning. And I always finished with how I never read an entire book from cover to cover.

By the time I hit sixth grade, I hated books the same way some kids hate monsters. Not because I thought they'd hurt me, but because I knew they already had.

Anytime the teacher called on me to read in front of the class, my throat closed before my mouth even opened. The words blurred on the page, letters shifting and swimming like they were trying to escape. My palms would sweat so badly that the thin paper stuck to my fingers. It wasn't just nerves. It was muscle memory. My body still believed that getting the words wrong meant punishment. That hesitation meant danger.

The classroom itself became a trap: the scrape of chairs on linoleum, the smell of pencil shavings and chalk dust, the sound of the clock ticking far too loud. When the teacher's voice floated down the rows, "Let's go around the room, each of you take a paragraph," my stomach dropped. I used to count ahead the number of people in front of me, quietly, when the teacher wasn't looking, trying to predict which paragraph would be mine to read aloud. Then I'd mouth the words under my breath, trying to memorize the hard ones before my turn came.

I practiced sounding confident, smooth, like I could read quickly and well. I tried to mimic the cadence of the kids who never seemed to flinch. If I could just get through my paragraph without stumbling, maybe she'd move on to the next person, and I could disappear again.

But sometimes, even when I read every word right, the heat in my face wouldn't fade. I could still feel the ghost of his voice in my head, correcting, criticizing, demanding. The classroom wasn't his kitchen, but my body didn't know the difference. Every sentence still felt like a test I was destined to fail.

In my sixth-grade reading class, reading had turned into a scoreboard. My teacher—cold, sharp, and always looking for someone to make an example of—announced at the start of the year that we had to read one thousand pages per marking period. Four thousand pages total for the school year. She made it sound like a punishment in my ears, a measurement of worth disguised as homework.

Newbery Medal winners and other "special" books counted double, but to me they were all the same; dry, joyless stories about people I didn't care about, written for kids who didn't flinch when words became weapons. Every title on the poster board at the front of the room felt like a threat. I'd look at those shiny covers: Bridge to Terabithia, Hatchet, Sounder, and feel nothing but dread. It wasn't the stories I hated; it was what they represented. Reading meant exposure. Reading meant failure. Reading meant that same invisible test I could never seem to pass, no matter how hard I tried to sound normal.

A few weeks before the first marking period ended, she called me out in front of everyone during class. "Zero pages," she said, her voice slicing through the room like a paper cut. "Everyone else has nearly finished their thousand. You haven't read a single one. I will not hesitate giving you an F."

Different room, different adult, same test I could never pass.

All the writing assignments I'd done in my journal, all the testing scores, the homework; none of it mattered to her. The only thing that counted was what I hadn't done, the defiance she imagined in my silence. I could tell she'd been waiting for the moment to pounce, to prove that fear worked better than encouragement.

I remember the heat crawling up my neck, the way the air seemed to hold its breath. The class went silent in that special kind of silence kids make when they smell someone else's shame. She just stood there, staring at me like I'd done something unforgivable, waiting for me to defend myself.

"If you don't start reading soon," she said, "you'll get an F."

I don't remember what I said back or if I said anything at all. I just remember the weight of her stare, the feeling of being exposed and small, and the quiet humiliation that sank into my bones now that everyone in the class knew my struggle. My ears rang. My vision tunneled. I wanted to disappear into the desk, into the floor, into anywhere but there.

I wanted to fake the page count and submit it. God, I wanted to. Everyone else seemed to glide through their books; some even bragged about padding their numbers, flipping through pages they hadn't read and writing down inflated totals. Thinking back now, maybe that would have been the smartest way forward. But I couldn't do it.

I was too nervous she'd quiz me on the story, the way my dad used to when I read too fast at home. I could still see him leaning over me, testing my recall, catching any word I stumbled on, his voice rising with every mistake. In my mind, getting caught lying was worse than getting an F. At least an F only went on paper. His punishments lasted longer.

So instead of making something up, I sat there with my stomach in knots, dreading the next time she'd call on me, trapped between my hatred of reading and my fear of being exposed. Every day that passed without turning in the assignment made the knot tighter, until the anxiety itself became another form of study.

It wasn't a threat, and she meant it. That marking period ended with an F in reading. Not a low B or a C. An F in reading, as if my entire effort in that class had been erased because I hadn't filled out the page count. The rest of my report card glowed: A's, a few B's. But that F sat there like a stain I couldn't scrub off, proof that failure could find me even when I'd done everything I could to avoid it.

I remember it was Friday after school. My mom got home and we had a quick dinner to hold me over since it was my dad's weekend. He was picking me up on his way home from work, which usually happened around 6:30 p.m. He knocked on the door and I answered it.

My mom had mentioned that report cards were sent out earlier that week, and that I'd done exceptionally well in everything except reading—"a teacher who seems to have a vendetta against Jeff," was how she put it, her voice protective, almost apologetic.

When she said it, he laughed; a sharp, dismissive sound. "Oh come on, teachers don't have vendettas against kids," he said, like it was the most ridiculous thing he'd ever heard.

Then she showed him the report card.

I watched his face shift. For a split second, there it was; real anger, hot and quick, cutting through the mask. His eyes locked on the red F, and I could see the calculation behind them. But as fast as it came, it was gone. He smoothed it over with a small, practiced smile, the kind he used when he knew he had an audience. My mom was standing right there, and he wasn't about to lose control in front of her.

He looked angry when he saw me, but he said nothing. His jaw was tight, his eyes scanning me the way someone looks for evidence of wrongdoing before the crime has even happened. We got in the truck, buckled up without a word, and he just drove, away from the peace of my mother's house, around a few corners, into a silence that felt deliberate.

Something was wrong. He was never quiet unless he was asleep, or planning something. The silence wasn't relief; it was strategy. It filled the space between us like fog, thick and waiting. The hum of the engine and the rhythmic click of the turn signal were the only sounds, steady and mechanical, masking everything that wasn't being said.

The air in the truck felt heavy, too still, the kind that presses on your chest even when you're breathing fine. I tried to make small talk: something about school, maybe about a TV show I'd watched the night before, his plans for this weekend. Anything to break the tension. But he stayed wordless, staring straight ahead, his knuckles pale against the steering wheel.

He didn't have to raise his voice to make me feel small. He knew silence worked better. He always knew that if he waited long enough, I'd start talking first. I couldn't stand the kind of quiet that felt like a trap, like a staring contest I could never win. My throat would tighten, and I'd start to fill the space with words just to make it stop; words that would, somehow, always turn against me.

Then, without any warning, he slammed on the brakes in the middle of a main road. Tires screeching, seat belts snapping tight, the world lurching forward all at once. My chest hit the strap so hard it took my breath away. The truck shuddered to a violent stop, the nose dipping, the sound of rubber tearing against pavement echoing through my ribs.

For a heartbeat, everything froze. Then came the noise: horns erupting behind us, angry, overlapping blasts; the whine of tires as cars swerved into the opposite lane to avoid crashing into us. A blur of color—red, white, silver—sped past the windows. The smell of burnt rubber filled the air, acrid and hot.

He turned toward me quickly, the movement too fast for what came next.

"AN F?!" he shouted, his voice exploding inside the small cabin, each word a grenade. "AN F, ARE YOU SERIOUS? YOU GOT AN F?"

He leaned closer, his face inches from mine, demanding the answer he already knew. "LOOK ME IN THE EYES! WHAT DID YOU DO? HOW COULD YOU DO SO BAD?"

His breath hit my face—sour, hot, furious. His eyes bulged, the whites veined and wet. His bottom teeth jutted over his top lip, spit collecting at the corners of his mouth. I could see the pulse hammering in his neck, the way his jaw trembled not from fear, but from restraint that might give out any second.

He kept screaming for me to look at him—"LOOK ME IN THE EYES WHEN I'M TALKING TO YOU!"—but my gaze kept darting everywhere else. The passenger-side mirror. The flashing headlights behind us. The drivers swerving past, staring. The world outside was a blur of motion and noise, but inside the car, everything was too sharp. His face. His hands strangling the steering wheel. His rage, alive and feral, filling every inch of space between us.

I can still see that burgundy-and-tan Isuzu Trooper II, the tan interior glowing under the setting sun, the stick shift jutting up like a weapon between us. I can still feel the moment suspended there in the middle of the road, horns blaring, cars squeezing past, his breath in my face, his eyes so wide they seemed ready to burst.

And then, just as suddenly as it began, he turned forward again. The world lurched back into motion. He started driving. Silent now, both hands clamped around the wheel, his jaw tight enough to crack a tooth. The engine whined as he shifted, the road humming beneath the tires, but the real noise was the silence; thick, humming, dangerous. I could feel the anger radiating off him like heat from a stove, the kind you can't see but still flinch away from.

He didn't yell anymore. He didn't have to. The silence after the storm was worse than the noise. It was the kind of quiet that hummed in your ears, the kind that made every small sound feel dangerous.

"Well," he finally said, his voice low and clipped, each word sharp enough to cut, "I guess you need to do even more reading now."

He knew I hated reading. He knew exactly what it did to me, how the words knotted up in my throat, and how my hands shook when he watched me. And since I wasn't reading enough at my mom's house, he made sure I read for an hour every visit at his. That amount of horrible reading time was about to go up. I could already feel it.

I didn't say anything. I just nodded, hoping that agreeing would make it end faster. My stomach ached from holding everything in. I wanted out of that car. I wanted out of his house. I wanted out of his reach. I just wanted to leave.

I turned my face toward the window and watched the neighborhood blur past. My breath fogged the glass, and I started tracing shapes with my finger to distract myself. We weren't far from my mom's house yet; if I opened the door now, I could probably make it. I pictured it: the handle lifting, my feet hitting the pavement, the rush of cold air in my face as I ran. I saw myself cutting across lawns, darting between mailboxes, walking the rest of the way home.

But I knew he'd chase me. I knew he'd grab my arm, maybe harder than he meant to. I knew the sound of his shoes on asphalt. No matter what, I'd still end up at his house with him.

When we finally pulled into the driveway, my whole body was buzzing. I could feel the engine still vibrating through the seat, my pulse keeping the same rhythm. He turned it off, threw the truck into first, yanked the keys out, and slammed the door like it had insulted him. I followed behind, slow, hoping he'd go inside first so I could have a second to breathe.

He didn't keep it private. Of course he didn't. The moment the door opened with that familiar, haunting squeak, he announced it to everyone like he was giving a speech.

"Jeff got an F in reading!" he declared, voice booming through the hallway. "An F! Can you believe that?"

He said it like it was headline news, like he was proud to be the one breaking the story, trying to incite a response from them and staring at me for my reaction. My stepsister—my age, gifted classes, honors, the one who loved reading for fun—laughed. Not a cruel cackle, but the kind of laugh that still lands like a punch when you're already on the floor. It was the kind of sound that reminds you you're different, that everyone else belongs except you.

I hated that laugh. I hated the whole scene and the way everyone looked at me, like I'd done something wrong just by existing. I hated that fucking house, the smell of dust and cats, the piles of junk in the corners, the rooms filled with his noise and his anger.

And more than anything, I hated my father. I hated him for the rage, for the silence, for the way he made even reading feel like punishment. I hated him for the way he made me feel, like every movement, every breath, was something I had to monitor. Like love was a test and I'd already failed it.

For some reason, I never felt safe with him. Even when he wasn't yelling, even when the air was still, there was something coiled in him that made my skin stay alert. It was in the way his voice could shift without warning, how calm could turn to fury before I even realized what I'd done wrong. He didn't have to hit to make me afraid; my body did the math for me.

My heart would race before he spoke. My stomach would tighten when his footsteps echoed down the hall. My shoulders would rise without thinking, bracing for something that might not even come. Those weren't choices; they were reflexes; small, invisible flinches my body learned to perform to keep me safe.

It's strange, looking back, how early the body learns danger. Before language. Before logic. I didn't have words for abuse or control back then. I just knew what fear felt like when it lived under your skin. My muscles understood long before my mind did.

Being around him felt like holding my breath for hours. I could never quite exhale. Even when he was kind, even when he laughed, I'd wait for the turn. Because there was always a turn. The way he smiled never quite reached his eyes; the way his praise always carried a catch. I'd stand there, nodding, pretending I believed it, pretending not to notice the quiet thrum of dread beneath it all.

And maybe that's what I hated most. Not the yelling, not even the silence, but the waiting. The waiting for the shift. The constant scanning for clues that it was coming again. The ache of knowing that peace, in that house, was never really peace at all.

Chapter 3 – The VHS Tape That Should Have Saved Me

One of the earliest rules he ever taught me was about pain.

I was in sixth grade, sitting in the back seat on the right side of the car, legs bent neatly, feet on the floor mat. He was loading something long into the space beside the front seats, some awkward, heavy-looking object that wouldn't quite fit. It lurched forward suddenly, bumping against my shin. The tap was light, harmless, the kind of thing most people would laugh off. But the sound that came out of me wasn't laughter. It was instinct.

"Ouch," I said, automatic, small.

He froze. Then he turned and looked at me, his eyes sharp and dissecting, as if I'd said something offensive. "Don't say that unless you're actually hurt," he said. His voice wasn't loud, but it carried weight. "You said it without being hurt." Then, almost casually, he added, "Remember the boy who cried wolf."

The way he said it made the air in the car go still. I felt like I did something wrong, unsure whether to apologize. It hadn't really hurt, well not much, but that wasn't the point anymore. The real sting wasn't in my leg; it was in the correction. In that quick, surgical way of his, he turned a reflex into a rule, a feeling into a failure.

From that moment on, I learned to think before I reacted, to pause before every flinch. Even my body had to ask permission. I started measuring everything; tone, timing, even the sound of surprise, to make sure it wouldn't be used against me. I became fluent in stillness, skilled at pretending not to feel.

That's how it started: the quiet training that would one day make me second-guess my own hurt. It was never about the shin or the word. It was about control. And like most of his lessons, it worked.

The next rule was about blame.

My younger sister Anna had found the crayons I'd left on the kitchen table after using them for a project. She was little and curious and did what little kids do; she climbed up onto a chair, stretched across the table, and pulled herself toward the bin. Nobody stopped her. Nobody was watching. The crayons rolled and clattered, and she grabbed a handful, testing each color against the nearest open space. Within minutes, the family-room wall had become her canvas, a looping, bright mess of color in the corner, a tangle of reds and blues and greens about three feet by three feet.

When the adults saw it, I was marched down into the family room to look at the wall. The guilt came straight to me. You should've put the crayons away, they said. It didn't matter that nobody in that house ever put anything away; clutter was part of the air, part of the wallpaper, part of the way the house existed. The table was always full of half-finished things: old mail, empty mugs, tools that didn't belong there. But rules only applied when they could be used against me.

Anna was small, sweet-faced, and still in that golden age where mistakes were cute. She was quietly forgiven before she even knew forgiveness was needed. But for me, there was a lecture. There was always a lecture. Responsibility was a coat I wasn't allowed to take off, no matter how young I was, since there was always someone younger watching.

So I was punished for leaving the crayons out, and Anna was quietly forgiven for being small. I remember staring at the wall, the color still bright and cheerful, thinking how something that innocent could turn into proof of my failure. That house was chaos made permanent, and the mess was never just physical; it was moral, emotional, everywhere.

I remember deciding, even then, that if no one else could see it, I would make them see. Someday, I'd find a way to prove it to them. They had to see it.

That summer I borrowed my dad's camcorder, without his knowledge. I remember the clumsy weight of it in my hands, the black plastic, a strap that rubbed the back of my palm, how adult it felt to carry. I plugged it in to charge overnight, watching the tiny red-light blink and thinking it was an accomplice. I made a plan to get up early the next morning, before anyone else, when the house would be empty of adults and the other kids would still be asleep.

I practiced pretending to be asleep while the adults went room to room checking on older kids before they left for work. I heard shoes on the porch, the hollow sound of keys in the lock, the faint cough of the truck starting, and then the gravel crunching as the car rolled away down the driveway where the pavement faded to rocks. I waited until the last engine noise faded and the house sighed into a different kind of quiet. Then I grabbed the camcorder and slipped out of bed like a ghost.

I filmed everything while the house was mine. I worked methodically, the way detectives must. The hoarder bedrooms were the worst: piles of shirts and boxes packed so high that the ceiling felt closer. Closets had doors hanging off their tracks because too much was stuffed in; I filmed the door hinges trembling as I nudged the frame with my shoulder. The floors were layered with trash: old wrappers, magazines, soggy napkins, and the counters had no empty space anywhere you looked. I crept through each doorway, whispering into the lens so the tape would know where it was, narrating like I was making my own report. "This is the bedroom… this is the closet… this is the floor." My voice sounded small, but it steadied me.

The garage and basement were impassable mountains of junk. I could only get as far as the entrances without a clear path, so I panned slowly from the threshold, letting the camera drink in the piles: boxes labeled with years, stacks of yellowed legal papers, broken chairs half-buried in a sea of shopping bags. The dining room had been sealed off, the door shut against towers of paper and plastic, so I circled the hallway and used the other set of wooden doors to get in. The kitchen was sticky underfoot; each step made a faint tacky sound. Every inch of counter was buried: a jungle of dirty dishes, a crusted casserole dish, a jar with a spoon in it that had been left there for days. The living room, once a place to sit, had become a toy pit with plastic animals and batteries and broken plastic, but also alive with fleas. I could feel them land on my legs as I crouched; black dots leaping like punctuation across my skin. I zoomed in on them jumping on me.

Upstairs, the hallway carpet had vanished under clothes and blankets, the linen closet yawning open because it couldn't close over the things stuffed inside. Even the bathrooms were layered with grime; a domestic neglect so normalized that it didn't even register as wrong anymore. I filmed the little things, the details that made the rot real: the half-empty plastic cups of Coca-Cola abandoned on nightstands, green and white furry mold fuzzing the tops, the fizz long gone but the smell still sweet and sour. In the hallway, a cat had turned the linen closet into a nest; her litter of kittens mewled among towels that had toppled to the floor, tiny mouths searching for warmth in a pile that should have been clean.

I kept filming until the entire house was recorded by the lens. I fed the footage into the VCR using the included cables and recorded it onto a blank VHS tape carefully, with my finger on the power button if someone came into the room unexpectedly. Then after I verified the VHS tape was good, I recorded over the camcorder tape itself, covering the lens with the black protector so what I'd filmed wouldn't be obvious if he ever checked it. I rewound the tape back to the end of the last thing recorded, which felt like erasing evidence and replacing it with the future.

When I smuggled the VHS home, it felt like carrying contraband from a crime scene. My heart hammered so loud I was sure the tape would vibrate in my backpack. I wrapped it in a shirt and tucked it deep inside a hidden compartment, fingers fumbling as if the act of hiding might make the whole thing vanish. Before we got into the car to go back to my mom's, I rehearsed what I'd say if he ever found it—how I'd explain away the truth, how I'd pretend it was nothing more than curiosity, a school project gone wrong. I practiced my voice and the measured sentences I'd need to sound reasonable and mute.

But underneath the rehearsal was something harder: the certainty that the tape mattered. It was small and grainy and messy, but it was proof. If I could show it. If anyone would sit and watch and really see, then maybe the rules would change. Maybe the lectures would stop landing like blows. Maybe they'd have to face what they'd let happen, and I wouldn't have to go to that house anymore. That thought made my hands steady again, and for the first time, the plan actually felt like it might work.

The night I got home from his house, my mom sat on the couch to watch the tape. Her eyes went wide, her hand rising to cover her mouth. By the halfway mark she was crying, really crying, whispering how sorry she was that I ever had to stay there. She called my Nana that same night, and we drove straight to her house so she could see it. The next evening we took it to my mom's best friend's house so their family could watch and talk about it, and later that week, to my aunt and uncle's house on my mom's side. Nobody from my dad's side ever saw the tape or even knew it existed.

Each viewing felt like a small trial where the truth finally had a voice, and it was by my doing. I narrated live over the footage. "This is the kitchen. Look at the floor. That's the couch we have to sit on when we are forced to read aloud." People stared, stunned, and for the first time, I felt something close to vindication. I wasn't dramatic. I wasn't ungrateful. I wasn't crazy.

Before long, the tape became something of a spectacle at holidays and birthday parties. Relatives asked me to bring it so they could "finally see what it was like up there." I thought it would be evidence; something that would make people step in, call someone, maybe even get the house condemned so I wouldn't have to go back. But instead, they treated it like dark entertainment. They laughed in disbelief, horrified but detached, saying things like "I can't believe anyone could live like that." They weren't feeling sorry for me. They were feeling relieved that it wasn't them.

But, I was finally believed.

I'd handed them a piece of my pain, neatly packaged on a VHS tape, and they turned it into conversation. Into gossip. Into something to play between dinner and dessert. And when it was over, they handed it back with pity and a shake of the head. "That's just how he is, disgusting" someone said.

That sentence burned hot. Because it meant the truth didn't matter, not if it was inconvenient, and not if it required them to act. The evidence was there, in grainy detail, and they all looked away.

Nobody called anyone. Nobody stopped the visits. Nobody asked how it felt to sleep in that house or breathe that air or wake up knowing I'd have to go back again. They had seen the truth, and still decided it wasn't their problem.

The tape disappeared into a drawer somewhere; forgotten like the rooms it showed. And I kept going back, weekend after weekend, pretending I hadn't seen what I'd recorded, pretending the smell of mold didn't cling to my clothes when I came home.

After that, everything was normal again, at least on the surface. Nobody mentioned the tape. It was as if the truth had been a dream that didn't survive daylight. My mom and I kept talking about it, even though we were powerless.

But I hadn't dreamed it. I could still see every frame when I closed my eyes: the piles, the stains, the litter of objects that told the story adults didn't want to read. I had shown them proof, and somehow, I was still the only one who couldn't look away.

At school that week, I remember sitting through class with a dull ache in my chest, trying to figure out how everyone else could seem so untouched by the world. I watched other kids pass notes, laugh, tap their pencils; kids who didn't have a second life in a house that felt like rot and shame with a controlling monster as king. Nobody at school knew where I went every other weekend. Nobody ever asked.

What cut deepest wasn't the house itself, it was that everyone knew and still sent me back. They had seen the fleas jumping, the couch turned brown, the filth you could smell even through a television screen. They had gasped, shaken their heads, cried a little, and then decided it was easier to do nothing.

That's the thing about neglect: it doesn't just happen in the house where it starts. It happens in the living rooms where people watch and look away. It grows in the space between what they saw and what they chose to forget.

So, I learned to forget, too. Or at least to act like I had. I learned to sit still when something hurt, to say I was fine, to nod when adults told me how "resilient" and "patient" I was. I learned that survival sometimes looks like silence.

But deep down, a part of me kept that tape running. Even now, when I think about that day, I can still hear the soft whir of the camcorder, the hush of my own breath as I filmed, the small defiant heartbeat behind every frame.

Because that was another day I found my voice, quiet, shaky, hidden in a backpack, but mine all the same. Still, I held on to one small victory. I had filmed it. I had made the invisible visible. For one day, the silence broke.

And in a house where I wasn't allowed to say ouch, I had finally screamed.

But I never forgot what that tape taught me; that people can watch a child's suffering on screen, documented, and still do nothing. That truth alone isn't enough to make anyone care.

What I didn't understand then, but can see now, is how early my dad began training me out of my own signals.

Saying "ouch" wasn't about a scrape or a bruise. It was a reflex, the body's way of saying something startled or hurt me, something didn't feel right. He couldn't stand that sound because it forced him to acknowledge cause and effect: that he did something and I reacted. So, he redefined pain to fit his comfort. It didn't matter if I was actually hurt; what mattered was whether he thought I should be.

That small correction planted something lasting: doubt. Doubt in my body's messages. Doubt in whether I was allowed to react. Over time, I learned to hesitate before every word, to replay moments in my head before they finished happening. The lesson was clear. If something didn't hurt enough, I must be overreacting. If I was upset, I must be the problem.

That's how emotional control works when it's disguised as "teaching." It starts small, with one forbidden word.

The house itself was another kind of teacher. It showed me that people could live in filth and still pretend everything was fine.

Every pile of junk, every sticky counter, every room sealed off from visitors was a kind of denial turned physical. It wasn't just a dirty house; it was the evidence of how much effort went into keeping up appearances instead of keeping up basic care.

And because he was a man who cared more about how things looked than how they were, the mess became my fault too, even though I was barely ever there; just like the crayons, just like the word "ouch."

When I filmed that tape, I didn't have language for trauma or gaslighting. I only knew that what I was seeing didn't match what the adults insisted was normal. That tape wasn't rebellion; it was self-defense. It was proof that I wasn't crazy, that the smell of decay and neglect was real, and that I wasn't inventing the crawling feeling under my skin when I sat on their stained couch and the cloth felt greasy and slightly damp.

Showing it to my mom, to Nana, to my aunt and uncle, it was the first time the truth had an audience.

And for a brief moment, I felt powerful.

Not powerful in the way he was, through intimidation and control. But through evidence. Through truth. I had turned my shame into something visible. And that visibility, more than anything, was what he feared.

Even more years later, I still feel that same pull between silence and proof. The part of me that still wants to whisper *ouch* whenever something stings, and the other part that stops me, scanning for permission.

That's what he left behind. Not just the mess, or the rules, or the fleas, but a nervous system that still double-checks whether pain is valid before it's spoken.

And the truth is, it always was.

Chapter 4 – J-Bird

I don't remember when the arm thing started. Maybe it was just a nervous habit, or something my body invented before my brain had language for comfort. It began quietly, without plan or thought. When the world got too loud, or the air in the room turned to static, I'd slide my hands under the same armpit on each side, fingers and knuckles pressed against my ribs, elbows locked tight to my sides. The pressure steadied me. It wasn't a hug; it was containment. A way to keep my insides from spilling out when everything else felt like it might. The warmth beneath each arm became a quiet shelter, a signal that I was still here, still whole, even if the rest of me felt scattered.

Dad noticed, of course. He noticed everything that made me different.

At first it was just a smirk. Then it became a show. "Look at J-Bird," he'd say, flapping his elbows once or twice for the audience, his brothers, his friends, whoever happened to be standing nearby. "Doesn't even need a coat; he's got wings."

They'd laugh, the kind of easy laughter that fills rooms without thinking. I'd laugh too, or at least twist my mouth into something that looked like it. But inside, I was folding in on myself. Every laugh taught me to shrink a little more, to tighten my elbows, to make myself smaller before anyone else could.

Soon everyone used the nickname. Aunts, uncles, cousins. I was J-Bird at picnics, J-Bird in Christmas cards, J-Bird in stories retold at family dinners. The name followed me like a leash. It fluttered after me even when he wasn't there to pull it.

I kept my arms straight after that. I practiced looking relaxed when I wasn't. I learned how to stand with my hands in my pockets or at my sides so no one could accuse me of hiding inside myself again. I taught my body not to comfort itself.

Still, every now and then, I'd catch myself doing it. Standing in his family room after some minor explosion, like the crayon incident, hands back under my armpits before I even realized it. I can see it clearly: the wax smell of the crayons, the big patch of color on the wall, the way the light hit it like a spotlight on guilt. He decided it was my fault. End of story.

The wall got scrubbed eventually, the punishment handed down, and I stood there, arms tucked tight, staring at a spotless square of drywall that might as well have been a warning sign. That's when I learned truth didn't have to be real to be believed. It only had to sound like him.

That nickname was used by almost everyone in his family. Even when I wasn't doing the arm thing anymore, the sound of it fluttered around rooms like a loose feather; light, harmless to everyone but me. It became his shorthand for weakness, for anything too soft or uncertain.

And once you start believing your softness is something to mock, you start practicing ways to hide it. You start mistaking numbness for strength. You start thinking safety means stillness.

For a while, hiding worked. Then came the Saturday that split the house in two.

It was one of those weekends that already smelled like trouble—the kind where the air feels wrong before anything happens. I'd arrived the night before (Friday), helped clean up dinner, kept my head down. By lunch the next day, the kitchen looked like it always did: plates everywhere, half-empty glasses, a film of chaos that never really lifted between visits.

After we finished lunch, he decided the entire kitchen needed to be scrubbed top to bottom. Each of the seven kids got a station. Mine was the island.

I cleared it, wiped, stacked, straightened—doing exactly what was asked. When it gleamed and was clear of anything except the centerpiece, I slipped into the family room, hoping that finishing early might buy a few minutes of quiet. It didn't.

"Why doesn't Jeff have to help clean anymore?" someone called from the kitchen.

"I did my part," I said from the family room. It was true. The mess had been there long before I showed up that weekend, and my section—the island—was spotless. "Besides," I added, "it wasn't even clean when I got here last night. Maybe that's why it's taking everyone so long."

Dad's voice cut through the noise. "Get back in here. We clean as a family."

"No thanks," I said, keeping my tone even. "I finished what you told me to do."

That was all it took. The air went brittle—the way it always did when he was about to lose control. His footsteps hit the floor in sharp, deliberate thuds, each one louder than the last.

I could hear him crossing the kitchen, descending the two steps toward me, his jaw clenched tight, eyes bulging, his bottom teeth pressed over his top lip like he was holding something in that might break the room apart.

He didn't need to yell. He rarely did. His silence did the work. It filled every inch of the room, thick and dangerous. I could feel it building behind me like heat, the kind that makes the skin between your shoulder blades tingle before contact even happens. I wanted to move, to explain, to say something that might defuse it, but the words jammed somewhere between fear and pride.

Then he was there; too close, too fast, his presence heavy enough to tilt the air.

"We clean as a family. Get back in there," he said.

The words were low, but they cut through me like a shout. Then his hand, his right hand, was on the back of my neck. Not a grab for balance or attention. A clamp. Hard. Hot. Fingers digging on the side of my neck as he pushed me forward.

The movement was quick, practiced, almost efficient. He shoved me by the neck up the two steps and back into the kitchen, steering me like an object, not a person. My body stumbled forward under his hand, head tilted down, my vision catching flashes of the linoleum floor and the edge of the counter. I could feel every finger, each ridge of pressure on my neck, as if he were leaving a print beneath the skin.

He didn't have to say anything else. The grip said it all: conversation over.

The house had gone quiet except for the scrape of chairs and the faint rattle of dishes. Everyone saw. I felt their eyes on me; the small, stunned audience pretending to keep working. My face burned. I felt like the entertainment, the warning, the example.

Then it was over as suddenly as it started. His hand dropped. He turned away and walked back toward the stairs, his shoes clicking against the tile, slow and deliberate again, as if order had been restored.

After that, the world shrank to the rage in my head and the sound of my own breathing. I imagined telling him off, walking out, but my mom's house was thirty minutes away by car. I cleaned instead. I wiped surfaces that were already clean until it was easier to keep moving than to think.

He disappeared upstairs, like always, certain that control had been reestablished.

I didn't cry. I didn't make a sound. I just waited for the house to settle into that eerie quiet again; the kind that leaves room for a grudge to grow.

When it finally did, I checked to make sure he was still upstairs. Theresa was in her room above the garage—she couldn't afford to move out, so she paid rent and electric and had a real key lock installed on her door. When the coast was clear, I picked up the wall phone above the built-in desk, the same one he used for everything that mattered, and dialed my mom at home.

She answered on the first ring.

"I don't have time to talk. Dad put his hands on me and I'm done. Can you pick me up?" I whispered. "Bottom of the driveway. At midnight."

She didn't ask for details; just a sharp inhale and then, "Oh, Jeffrey…" Her voice rose with a fear she was trying to hide. "Of course I'll be there. I love you. Stay safe from whatever is happening until then."

I hung up, checked the line again, made sure no one had heard. The rest of the evening passed in a haze of dinner, dishes, and television, the kind of pretending that families mistake for peace. After dinner, I talked the other kids into sleeping in the tent that night and told them to ask my dad to set it up after we ate, since I wasn't going near him. He agreed and set up the tent for us.

I was so happy the plan was working, that I might sleep in my own bed that night instead of another night on a dirty mattress with no sheets.

After we set up the tent, kids spilled everywhere, laughing and dragging sleeping bags through the grass. We picked our spots like campers on borrowed land. It wasn't rebellion; it was distance I could finally breathe in. The grass was cool and damp beneath the nylon floor. I zipped the flap halfway and watched the kitchen lights fade, one by one. Every window that went dark made the air a little easier to swallow.

My stepbrothers, stepsisters, half-brothers, and half-sisters drifted off one by one, their breathing turning into the steady rhythm of sleep I couldn't reach. By ten-thirty, the tent was a nest of quiet bodies. I checked my fold-up, wind-up alarm clock—the one I'd synced with the microwave earlier that afternoon when the plan first formed in my head. Once the hands reached 11:50, I'd start walking towards the bottom of the driveway.

When the time came, I unzipped the flap and slipped into the cool fall air, pulling it closed slowly behind me so the others wouldn't stir. The night air bit at my arms. The yard was silent except for the hum of insects and the occasional chirp that seemed too loud. I cut across the backyard, hugging the shadowed side of the house, careful to stay clear of the seven windows belonging to my father's bedroom.

The gravel underfoot was louder than I expected; each step cracked the night open like breaking glass. I was hoping the dog wouldn't hear and start barking. The moon hung low behind a thin veil of clouds, throwing just enough light to trace the outline of the driveway but not enough to see what might be waiting in the dark. I kept my eyes on the faint strip of silver where the gravel met the grass, heart pounding, every sound amplified.

The forest that flanked both sides of the drive felt alive. Crickets hissed in the tall weeds. Something small; maybe a toad, maybe something worse rustled near my shoe, and I jumped, pulse hammering in my throat. I kept going, every nerve tuned to the possibility of movement. I couldn't see more than a few feet ahead. For all I knew, there could've been snakes or raccoons or anything else waiting on the path.

The fear was physical. It crawled up the back of my neck and settled in my shoulders. The night smelled like wet dirt and pine and something metallic; maybe fear itself.

The hill was steeper than I remembered. It wanted to pull me down faster than my legs could handle. I half-walked, half-slid, trying not to trip on loose stones. Somewhere in the middle, near the bend where cars always got stuck in the gravel, I heard a rustle in the woods; a much heavier sound this time, something shifting leaves and tall weeds. My breath caught. I stopped dead, eyes scanning the black tangle of trees, trying to see what had made it. Then instinct took over.

I ran.

Gravel sprayed behind me as I sprinted, shoes slipping, lungs burning. Branches snapped somewhere to my left, maybe echo, maybe not. I didn't look back. My breath tore out of me in ragged bursts until the sound of my footsteps swallowed everything else.

And then, finally, the ground smoothed into pavement near the bottom. The air opened up.

And there she was.

My mom's car sat at the corner, headlights off, engine idling low. She was standing outside, a Virginia Slim glowing between her fingers, arms open in the faint dashboard light. I ran the last few yards, and she caught me; no questions, no words, just the kind of embrace that said she already knew everything.

I told her everything exactly how it happened on the drive home. She was nervous, chain-smoking two, three more cigarettes. The smoke curled out the open window as we crossed back into her part of town, and for the first time all weekend, I could breathe.

At dawn, she called him. Her voice was steady. She told him I was safe at her house. He hadn't noticed I was gone; everyone in the tent was still asleep.

The next evening, just after dinner, his headlights swept across the front of our small townhouse. I felt the air change before my mother even opened the door. My stomach turned in that old familiar way, the kind of dread that made my skin feel two sizes too small. I wanted so badly not to have to go back. I kept thinking maybe this time, the neck grab would finally be enough, the thing that proved to everyone that I shouldn't have to. I kept waiting for the universe to agree with me.

He stood there with that soft tone he used when he wanted to sound reasonable. "Can I talk to him for a minute?" he asked. Mom looked at me, then stepped aside. She shouldn't have had to make that choice, but she did what mothers in impossible positions do; she tried to keep the peace. He told her he just wanted to check that I was all right, that he wouldn't stay long. Then he asked if we could talk alone. She nodded, but she didn't go far. She was just in the kitchen, close enough to hear through the hallway. She always stayed close when he was around.

He sat across from me at the table like we were in a meeting, hands folded, voice calm. "Are you okay?" he asked first, and for half a second, I almost believed he meant it. The way he looked at me; steady, gentle, pretending concern, it was the same look he used on judges, on clients, on women who didn't know better yet. I said yes.

Then came the tilt. "Why did you leave? Do you know how scared everyone was when they woke up and you were gone?" His eyes locked on mine, the concern already hardening into accusation.

I said I couldn't stay, that he'd scared me when he got physical, and that I just wanted to go home.

He blinked, slow and disappointed. "You can't just walk away from your responsibilities, Jeff. You were the oldest. Those kids look up to you. What if something bad had happened? You can't abandon them like that."

The words landed heavy and absurd. Responsibilities. I was in middle school. He was the adult—drinking upstairs while seven children slept outside in a tent. Yet somehow, I was the one being scolded for leaving. It was like watching him rearrange the truth in real time, the same way he'd always rearranged furniture: loud, sudden, without warning.

He kept talking about how worried he'd been, how lucky it was that nothing terrible happened to any of the kids, how next time I should come to him if I felt upset. His voice was smooth, controlled, the kind that could convince anyone who hadn't seen the other side of him. It was an impressive rewrite: the man who caused the fear now playing the role of the protector.

I remember glancing toward the kitchen doorway, seeing just the edge of my mom's shadow and knowing she was still there, listening. She didn't interrupt, didn't shout him down, but she stayed there at the corner, like a quiet line of defense, like a witness who didn't need to take notes.

He stood to leave eventually, adjusting his jacket like he'd just finished a long day's work. "I just wanted to make sure you were all right," he said, as if that were the purpose all along.

Then he thanked my mom for letting him come inside and walked out into the night like a man who'd done a good deed.

Only after the car pulled away did Mom come back into the room. She didn't say much; just put her hand on my back and asked if I wanted some iced tea. But the way she looked at me said everything: I heard. I believe you. You're safe here.

Looking back now, I can see how ordinary those moments must have seemed to anyone else: an odd nickname, a spotless wall, a kid sleeping out in the backyard planning an escape. On the surface, it all could have passed for family life: teasing, chores, camping. But under it was a lesson plan in obedience.

That's how control works. It doesn't arrive as thunder; it starts as drizzle. A joke at your expense, a rule that changes mid-sentence, a silence that lasts long enough for you to fill it with apology. You learn early which version of yourself earns peace and which one earns punishment. By the time the real storms come, you've already built your shelter inside yourself—and mistaken it for safety.

The "J-Bird" thing was supposed to be funny. To him, it probably was. To everyone else, it was just a nickname that stuck. But for me, it became shorthand for the part of myself that wasn't allowed to exist: the nervous, soft, too-sensitive part. I didn't know it then, but every laugh chipped away at something private. I still catch myself folding my arms across my chest when I'm anxious, as if my body remembers before my mind does.

When I think of that night, the tent, the gravel, the breath I held until I saw my mother's car; I realize how young I was to already understand escape. I wasn't running from punishment that time; I was running toward proof that someone would still come for me. That single ride down the driveway changed something fundamental. From then on, I knew rescue was possible, even if it had to come from me.

I don't know if the arm thing was a disorder, a tic, or instinct. Maybe it was my body's earliest language for help. What I know is that it started as comfort and ended as shame. Somewhere between the first laugh and the last stomp, I stopped holding myself to feel safe and started doing it to stay small. And even now, years later, part of me is still learning the difference.

Maybe that's why, after that night, his control changed shape. It stopped coming at me as talking and started arriving as rules about who I was allowed to be. He wanted obedience that looked like normalcy; a version of me that proved he was a good father. And for a long time, I tried to give it to him, because pretending was safer than being myself.

Soon it wouldn't be about cleaning or chores at all, but about how I dressed, what I played, who I was allowed to be; and who I wasn't. The lessons were getting sharper now, the silences longer. The small storms had done their work. And though I didn't know it yet, the worst of his techniques—the ones that left no visible marks—were still waiting to begin.

Chapter 5 – Bloodlines and Punchlines

Weddings were supposed to be about family.

In ours, they were about theater.

My cousin's wedding was held in a reception hall that smelled faintly of old carpet and hairspray; the kind of scent that clung to you hours after you left. The open bar was the real centerpiece, a magnet for the loudest relatives. I was a teenager then. Awkward, quiet, and already perfecting the art of disappearing in a crowd and sidestepping the uncles who looked at me too long. My father was in full performance mode: tailored suit, polished shoes, that fixed smile that never quite reached his eyes. It was the look he wore when he wanted the world to see how normal we were, and how much money we had to prove it.

The whole family had come; the uncles with their big voices, the aunts with their practiced politeness, cousins I haven't seen in months. For most people, weddings are reunion and celebration. For me, they were surveillance. Every conversation was an evaluation; every look, a measurement.

Dinner was loud, the kind of loud that made me shrink in my chair. My father and his brothers traded jokes that weren't really jokes. Half were about politics; the other half about drinking. Every punchline ended with someone's laughter and someone else's silence.

After dinner, when the music started, I slipped away from the table. Everyone else was on the dance floor, and I wouldn't be caught dead there. I wandered toward the open bar instead to grab a soda, and that's when I heard them. Three of my uncles, huddled nearby, drunk and laughing really loud.

Uncle Mike said, "There's a fag in the bathroom." The other two looked up, waiting, and he grinned. "Let's go kill him." Their laughter came fast—short, jagged bursts that cut through the music and stayed ringing in my ears as I passed. I couldn't tell if it was a joke meant for me to overhear or if cruelty was just their native language.

I kept walking, heart thudding, pretending I hadn't heard. But the words followed anyway, clinging like smoke.

What would happen if they ever knew the truth about me?

Would I still be family?

Or just another story they'd laugh about after the next round of drinks?

I walked over to one of my cousins and slipped into her conversation, pretending nothing had happened, and that I hadn't just heard a drunk homophobe threaten violence for sport. A few minutes later, the DJ announced the father-daughter dance was starting. My father clapped along, his smile perfectly timed, the picture of proud kinship.

The night faded like all family events did: music, drinks, polite goodbyes. But the words I'd overheard didn't fade with it. They hung around, quiet but alive, surfacing at every gathering after that. It was never just one night; it was a language that kept repeating itself in new scenes, new voices.

At a different family party, someone's birthday celebration, Uncle Mike (the same one who'd joked about killing the gay man in the bathroom at the wedding) cornered me near the front door. "You like girls yet?" he asked, elbowing me in the ribs. The question came out of nowhere, casual enough to sound harmless to anyone listening, but to me it felt like a test.

"Yeah… starting to," I muttered, keeping my eyes on the floor.

He grinned, satisfied. "Good," he said, already turning away.

He walked off, leaving me standing there with a smile I couldn't drop fast enough. Moments like that didn't end when they were over; they lingered, finding new ways to show up at the next family gathering. And there was always another gathering.

Months later, it was New Year's Day, the one tradition that never changed: pork and sauerkraut at Uncle Mike's house for good luck for the upcoming new year. He cooked it every year, and the smell alone—savory and sharp, filling every room—was enough to make people forget whatever grudges had been carried over from Christmas.

I stood at the kitchen doorway while he worked, moving between pots, tasting and stirring like a man running his own restaurant. My dad was just around the corner in the hallway, close enough to hear but pretending not to listen. Uncle Mike said something to me; small talk, maybe a question, but what I remember was him watching my reaction. Then, mid-sentence, he smirked and said, "I'm so straight, I can't even eat the little white string inside eggs. I have to pull it out first."

I froze, trying to decipher what that meant. Was it another test, another performance, another way to signal what was acceptable? Before I could react, my father appeared from around the corner and said, almost impatiently, "C'mon, Mike," redirecting the conversation as if he could erase the moment by changing the subject.

For years I replayed that split second of intervention, wondering if he'd done it for me or for himself. Did he see the panic in my face, or did he just not want the conversation turning into gossip that might reach him later?

Either way, the message was clear: even my safety depended on his control.

That night, as the adults drank and laughter grew louder and looser, I sat near the edge of the room, tracing the patterns in the carpet with my eyes. Every so often, someone would ruffle my hair or ask about school. I smiled, nodded, answered politely, doing everything expected of me while trying to pack away what I couldn't yet name. I didn't have the words for it then, but I knew something was wrong.

In our family, cruelty came disguised as culture.

Jokes about women, about "real men," about who belonged; they were rituals, not conversations. Each one reinforced the hierarchy: men on top, emotions underneath, anything soft or uncertain crushed before it could form a shape.

When my father stepped in to stop Uncle Mike, he wasn't rejecting that hierarchy. He was guarding it.

He didn't want anyone else controlling the narrative of his son.

That privilege belonged to him alone.

Driving home that night, the car was quiet. I stared out the window, the road glowing faintly under the headlights. The air smelled of remnants of sauerkraut leftovers in the back. My father tapped his foot on the floor, humming along to a song on the radio.

The next morning, I woke up with that same heaviness I used to feel whenever I arrived at his house for visitation. Only this time, it wasn't about playing a role for him. It was about existing in a world that had already decided what I should be.

Every time someone asked if I liked girls, I felt that same sick weight in my stomach. Every time a man laughed too loudly, I heard those drunken homophobic voices again.

That weekend didn't just show me what my family thought about people like me, it showed me how easily love could turn into violence if you were born on the wrong side of their definition of normal.

The older I get, the more I realize that no one ever says, this is the moment you start hiding. It happens quietly, somewhere between a joke and a glance, a laugh that lasts a beat too long.

That night at the wedding wasn't the first time I'd felt unsafe around people who claimed to love me, but it was one of the first times I understood what that fear cost me. It taught me to translate everything before I spoke: every word, every gesture, every silence. I learned to measure myself against the temperature of the room, to predict when a sentence might turn into a weapon.

For a long time, I thought that was just growing up. Everyone has to learn how to fit in, right? But this wasn't fitting in; it was erasing. Each joke, each test, each half-smile of approval pressed me flatter against the wall until I wasn't sure there was anything left to press.

I envied people who could move through the world without editing themselves. I watched classmates joke and flirt and throw careless words into the air like confetti. Their freedom looked ordinary. Mine was conditional, a permission slip that could be revoked the moment I forgot my lines.

When I remember those family gatherings now, what stands out isn't just the words; it's the choreography. The men in one circle, louder with every drink. The women cleaning dishes, smiling tight. The children floating between rooms, learning which version of themselves to present. Cruelty wasn't an accident; it was tradition, passed down like recipes and last names.

And yet, there were moments of almost-tenderness that confused me more than the cruelty. My father refilling someone's glass. An uncle slipping me a twenty "for gas." The same hands that hurt could offer a gesture that looked like care. That was the trap. It kept me hoping that if I just behaved, the kindness would outweigh the rest.

Looking back, I can see how control masquerades as love. It promises safety while slowly teaching you that safety depends on obedience. My father's version of protection always came with that price tag. The minute he told Uncle Mike to stop, he reclaimed authority. Not to defend me, but to make sure no one else could decide the limits of my humiliation. He wanted the exclusive rights to it.

For years, I confused that control with care. I told myself that any parent would step in if things went too far. I even tried to convince myself he'd been proud of me that night, that maybe I'd finally done something right by staying quiet and polite. That illusion lasted until the next time he turned silence into a punishment. Then I understood: in our house, peace wasn't the absence of conflict, it was the pause between performances.

Sometimes I wonder what my life would have looked like if someone in that wedding hall had said, "That's not funny." Just one person. Maybe it would have changed nothing. Or maybe it would have cracked the surface enough for me to see a way out sooner. Most families have one relative who breaks the pattern, the one who sees it for what it is. In ours, no one wanted the role. The laughter was easier.

It's strange how the smallest details stay sharp when the big picture fades. I can still smell the vinegar of the sauerkraut mixing with the cold outside air. I can still hear my father's foot on the floor in the car, tapping to the rhythm of a song he liked. Those sensory scraps are how my brain stores danger—proof that it happened, even if I try not to revisit it.

I used to replay that drive home and imagine different endings. In one, he tells me he's proud of me. In another, he admits he doesn't know how to be the father I need. The truth is simpler and harder: he probably didn't think about it at all. For him, the night was a success. No scene. No embarrassment. Just another holiday checked off the calendar.

For me, it was the beginning of a pattern that would take decades to unlearn: anticipating harm before it arrived, and calling that intuition. That skill still lives in me. It's how I read rooms, how I navigate conversations, how I know when to disappear. It's also why I now write. Putting these moments into words gives them shape, and once something has shape, it can't stay hidden forever.

Writing this chapter forced me to revisit every layer of those memories: the fear, the confusion, the numbness that came after. It reminded me how early shame entered the room and how efficiently it taught me to police myself. But it also reminded me that memory itself can be an act of defiance. Every time I tell this story, I'm saying I survived the joke. I'm still here.

If you grew up under the same kind of gaze, you know the exhaustion of constant translation, the need to sound normal, act normal, be normal, when "normal" was never meant to include you. Maybe you still find yourself laughing at things that make your stomach twist, nodding along when someone crosses a line, just to keep the peace. I understand. That reflex once kept me alive. It doesn't have to keep you silent.

Families like mine are built on stories that never get questioned. The problem is, silence lets those stories live forever. This book, this chapter, is my way of interrupting them. It's not revenge; it's record-keeping. The truth deserves oxygen.

Now, years later, I can look back at that boy tracing patterns in the carpet and want to tell him:

You're not wrong.

You're not weak for feeling afraid.

You don't have to keep performing to deserve love.

He wouldn't have believed me then, but I keep saying it now—for him, and for anyone still sitting at the edge of the room, trying to disappear.

What happened in my family wasn't unique. Versions of it happen everywhere, in kitchens and churches and locker rooms, wherever cruelty hides behind laughter. I tell it here so that maybe, when someone hears a similar joke, they'll be the one who says, "That's not funny," and mean it.

A note before the next chapter:

The story continues into a darker part of my father's world— where control stopped hiding behind jokes and began showing its teeth. Chapter 6 reveals what that looked like. If you need to pause here, please do. Take care of yourself before reading on.

Chapter 6 – Forced to Fit

All week I'd begged my mom to call my dad, to tell him I didn't want to play soccer like he was demanding. I sat at the kitchen table tracing circles on the placemat while she held the phone, whispering that she'd "try again." She always tried. Every time she did, he refused to listen.

"It'll be good for him," he told her, like I was a problem to be solved.

"He needs to learn teamwork."

"He just doesn't like being told what to do."

I was eleven, maybe twelve, and already knew that being told what to do was the only thing I was good at.

The truth was simpler: I didn't like sports. I already knew I liked boys. I didn't like shouting, whistles, or the smell of sweat and grass pressed into skin. I didn't like how every game seemed to come with a winner and a loser and a crowd waiting to decide which one you were. The whole thing felt like another test; one more chance to fail in front of people. I wanted video games, quiet things, computers, or anything that didn't involve being measured in public.

But he decided that boys needed sports the way plants needed sunlight, and no argument from my mom or tears from me could compete with that kind of certainty. His voice always carried the weight of fact, like the world bent to his opinions.

He said everyone else in the family was on a team playing a real sport, so I had to be too. "You'll thank me later," he promised, as if gratitude were inevitable once obedience kicked in.

I didn't even have a practice before my first game. Not one. No uniform fitting, no drills, no meeting the team; just a time, a place, and a command to show up with him. I'd missed all the weekday practices since I lived with my mom during the week and the field was forty minutes away, one way, on a school night. And I knew nothing about soccer, besides trying to kick the ball into the goal, and not being allowed to use my hands.

Saturday morning came gray and cold, the kind of air that smelled like wet dirt and felt like bad news. We were late, of course. He was always late. My mom always joked, "That man will be late to his own funeral somehow," and I remember hoping that would be true one day.

By the time we pulled into the gravel lot beside the field, other kids were already playing, chasing the ball up and down the grass. Parents lined the sidelines with folding chairs and travel mugs, their cheering sharp in the air. The smell of coffee and exhaust mixed with damp grass. He parked crooked, threw my gear bag toward me, and said, "Go. They need you out there."

My stomach twisted as I ran, the cleats too small, the socks sliding down. My breath puffed out in small clouds as I jogged toward the team, trying to look like I knew where I was supposed to be. The coach shouted something I couldn't understand—"Striker!"—and pointed toward the field. I nodded like I knew what that meant and sprinted to the center, pretending confidence, hoping no one could see the panic in my eyes.

For the first few minutes, I managed to blend in, jogging just behind the others, copying their movements, clapping when they clapped. I never wanted the ball to come near me. I wanted to look busy but invisible, helpful without risk. When the ball rolled close, I veered away, cheering for teammates like a spectator who'd wandered onto the field.

It didn't last. The other kids noticed.

"Kick it, kick it!" someone yelled.

Then louder: "What are you doing?"

Their faces changed—brows tightening, mouths hardening. The word striker finally reached me as accusation instead of instruction. The ball shot my way again, and this time I panicked and kicked—clean contact, the thud echoing off my shin guard—and sent it straight toward the wrong goal.

A whistle screamed.

Then voices.

"Wrong way!"

"Oh my God!"

"Idiot!"

It felt like all of them yelling at once, a chorus of disbelief. My body locked up. I froze, then kept running out of reflex, tears already burning behind my eyes. When the other team scored, the sound that followed wasn't celebration—it was humiliation, amplified through a dozen small throats.

I didn't want to cry in front of them, but the tears came anyway—hot, loud, unstoppable. I dropped my hands to my knees, gasping, the air jagged in my throat. I wanted to disappear, to sink into the ground and let the grass close over me. When I finally walked off the field, I could feel every set of eyes following me. The game kept going without me, which somehow hurt more.

He was standing near the sideline, hands in his jacket pockets, expression unreadable. I stood beside him, shaking, my face wet and burning. For a second I thought he'd kneel down or say it's okay, but he didn't. He watched the field like a man studying a traffic jam; annoyed, detached, waiting for it to clear.

I sobbed until there was nothing left to sob. My throat hurt. My face burned. The world blurred into streaks of green and white. Finally, he said, flat and final, "Let's go."

That was it. No lecture, no comfort, no anything.

We walked to the car in silence. The sound of my cleats crunching against the gravel was the only thing either of us said. The drive home smelled like grass and failure. He didn't speak until we were halfway there.

"We need to practice before next time," he said, as if the crying had been disobedience.

I stared out the window, counting telephone poles until the number lost meaning. The radio played quietly, but I remember the rhythm of it syncing with the thump in my chest.

There was never a next time. That was the first and last soccer game I ever played. He never mentioned it again, not directly. It vanished the way his failed experiments always did;

buried under new orders, new lessons, or new ways to make me prove something.

But the silence around it stayed. Every time I saw a field or heard a whistle, I felt that same helpless heat behind my eyes. Even now, I don't watch sports unless someone I love wants the company. Winning and losing still feel like traps.

That day taught me the rule beneath all his rules: it wasn't about learning or fun or health. It was about control dressed as encouragement, humiliation disguised as parenting.

And I thought the lesson would end there.

But his humiliation was only warming up. The next time it came, it didn't wear cleats. It came printed in black ink, folded neatly inside a newspaper he'd saved just for the occasion.

It was a Friday night, after dinner. I'd just arrived at the house. Theresa had picked me up from my mom's place that day, since she finished work around four. The house was loud in that familiar, chaotic way; plates clattering into the sink, the hum of conversation, kids arguing over who had to dry. It smelled like spaghetti sauce and lemon dish soap, the usual noise and motion of his kind of family life: messy, loud, performative.

I was at the counter wiping crumbs when Dad called my name from across the kitchen.

"J-Bird, come here a second," he said, his voice too casual to be casual.

The Philadelphia Inquirer sat on the island, open so deliberately it might as well have been staged. Later, I'd learn he'd driven an hour and a half home from the city with that paper on the passenger seat, waiting for this exact moment. He hadn't even folded it up. He wanted everyone in the kitchen—Theresa, her three kids, my three siblings, whoever else happened to be in earshot—to see what he was about to do.

"Look at this," he said, tapping the headline with one finger before reading it out loud to everyone nearby.

HAWAII LEGALIZES GAY MARRIAGE.

His voice carried that bright edge of excitement that only showed up when he thought he was about to prove a point, or make a joke at someone's expense.

He looked straight at me.

"You could always go there."

The room fell quiet so fast it felt like someone had turned off the air. The clatter stopped. The sink ran dry. Eight pairs of eyes turned toward me at once. I could feel the blood rush to my face, the hot, electric sting of being cornered in plain sight.

He smiled. An almost friendly smile, the kind that made strangers trust him.

"Right, Jeff?"

He let the words hang there, pretending it was humor. Everyone knew better. The way he said *you* was deliberate, weighted; the same tone he used in cross-examinations when he'd already trapped the witness. He wanted a reaction:

laughter, denial, anger, anything that would feed the performance.

I stared at the counter, tracing the grain of the wood beneath the edge of the newspaper, pretending to study it so I wouldn't have to meet anyone's eyes. My throat felt like it was closing. My skin was hot enough to burn. I wanted to disappear into the countertop, into the air, into anywhere but there.

Theresa's daughter giggled nervously, not understanding why. Theresa herself froze with a dish towel in her hand, eyes flicking between us like she was waiting for permission to breathe. No one said a word. Not one person intervened.

The silence stretched so long it became a second language. He was waiting for my response. I could feel it; the unspoken demand for performance.

Finally, I shrugged my shoulders and mumbled, "Why would I have to go there?" My voice cracked halfway through, small and strained. Then I walked to the other side of the kitchen, pretending to clean something that didn't need cleaning. I made sure to sound busy, to look straight, to move like someone who wasn't trembling inside. My cover story was obedience.

He folded the newspaper once, slowly, precisely, like a case file being returned to order. Then he walked away, satisfied.

That's how he liked to do it; humiliation as theater. He rarely raised his voice since he didn't have to anymore. He just created a scene, made sure there was an audience, and delivered his line. The silence that followed was applause enough.

The air in the room felt different afterward. Dense. Watching me had become a group activity. Every word I said, every pause, every movement carried new weight. He'd marked me in front of them all, and they knew it.

I didn't have the language for it then, but I understood the rules: when he joked, everyone else had to laugh. And if you didn't, you became the next joke.

That night stayed with me like a stain that wouldn't wash out. It was the first time he'd used my identity as a weapon; something to mock, something to expose, something to make the room laugh at before dinner was even cleared.

And that was the point. If he'd truly wanted to talk, he could have pulled me aside, spoken in private, asked if I was okay, or even just tried to understand. But he didn't want a conversation; he wanted an audience. That was his stage, and I was the exhibit.

He didn't bring it up again right away. He didn't need to. The silence afterward did the work, wrapping around my throat like a leash no one else could see. And after that night, I understood that my father didn't have to shout to make a spectacle; he could destroy you quietly, with charm, and still make sure everyone was watching.

The following weekend, he said we needed to "talk."

Those words were never an invitation. They were a warning.

It was Friday again and I just arrived from my mom's house, after dinner. Everyone else was drifting from the table toward the living room or heading upstairs to escape him. A few of the younger kids were laughing somewhere down the hall, the

TV just starting up. He stood by the island, arms crossed, wearing that same look he used before every ambush; steady, unreadable, already rehearsed.

"Sit down," he said.

I sat at the kitchen table.

He kept his eyes on me while pretending to sound concerned, the kind of faux sympathy that made people think he was patient. "Laura's worried about you," he began, lowering his voice like this was a private conversation, though the house wasn't truly empty. "She said you might be…" — he paused, savoring the pause — "a pedophile."

The word hit me like a slap. I actually blinked, like the air had cracked. My ears rang. For a second I thought I'd misheard him. But then I saw it—the faint, almost imperceptible smirk that twitched across his mouth. He'd enjoyed saying it.

"She's worried about you being around your little brother," he added, as if reading a line from a report he'd written himself.

The words didn't even make sense. My brother was just a little kid—five, maybe six. I was almost a teenager, still figuring out who I even was, still half-afraid of the dark. I didn't have the vocabulary to grasp what the accusation implied, only the sick heat in my chest that told me it was monstrous. And I knew, somehow, that he knew exactly what he was doing.

I stared at him, waiting for a sign that this was a joke, a test, anything. But there was no flicker of doubt in his eyes. Just satisfaction.

I felt my heartbeat climb into my throat. My skin buzzed. It was like he'd dropped a live wire into the room and stepped back to watch me shake.

I was heartbroken, but I couldn't show it. I wanted to believe Laura hadn't said it, that maybe he'd twisted her words the way he twisted everyone's. But deep down I knew the truth: whether she'd said it or not, he wanted it said. He wanted to poison the only other bond outside of that house that had ever felt safe.

My chest went cold. "That doesn't make sense," I managed to say, my voice small, distant, like it belonged to someone else. "I don't even know why she would say that."

He nodded slowly, pretending to be thoughtful, pretending to share my confusion. "She just worries. You know how she is." The lie rolled off his tongue so casually it almost sounded tender. Then, as always, he moved on, talking about chores, or school, or something meaningless, like the word pedophile hadn't just been fired into the air between us.

That was his genius: planting poison and walking away before it bloomed.

When Theresa came downstairs later, she acted like nothing had happened. "Anyone want dessert?" she asked, her voice too bright, brittle around the edges. I said no. My throat hurt. I couldn't swallow even water without feeling it burn.

That night, I lay awake listening to the house breathe; the pipes ticking, the floorboards settling, the hum of the refrigerator, and all of it sounded like accusation. Every creak felt like someone whispering behind a door. I kept replaying his words, wondering what Laura thought of me now, if she'd look at me differently, if my brother would too.

How do you tell your mother something like that? How do you say my father called me a pedophile without sounding broken? I didn't understand it fully myself. How do you describe a wound that leaves no mark? How do you explain the way someone can set a whole house against you with a single sentence?

When he drove me home that Sunday, he smiled as we pulled into the parking lot in front of the townhouse. "I'll see you in two weekends," he said. The same smooth, empty tone as always, like he'd just dropped me off from summer camp.

I nodded, walked inside, and went straight to my room. Mom called from the kitchen, asking how the weekend was.

"Fine," I said.

I didn't know how to explain the kind of wrong that hides inside silence.

That was the weekend I stopped believing that silence could keep me safe.

For years after, he'd drop little reminders—phrases he liked to repeat, just loud enough to sting.

"You know people talk."

Or, "Perception matters more than truth."

They weren't lessons. They were threats dressed as advice.

The soccer field had taught me how to fake confidence.

The newspaper taught me how to fake normal.

But that weekend taught me how to fake safety.

He could've pulled me aside in private if he truly believed any of it, if he'd cared to talk or ask or protect. But that wasn't the goal. This wasn't about worry; it was about isolation. He wanted me ashamed. He wanted me alone. And he knew exactly how to make that happen.

Looking back now, those memories no longer come in order. They arrive like a slideshow of humiliation: the soccer field, the newspaper, the accusation that still makes my stomach knot. The sequence doesn't matter. The feeling does: the tightening in my chest, the breath held too long, the certainty that whatever version of myself I offered was the wrong one.

That's how control works when it wears the mask of parenting. It teaches you to confuse obedience with love, fear with discipline, humiliation with guidance. At first it sounded harmless: You should toughen up. You should be like the other kids. You should play a sport. Each *should* sounded like opportunity, until it replaced *want* so completely that I forgot what wanting felt like.

The soccer field was my introduction to public failure. I learned what it meant to disappoint him in front of strangers. The newspaper was my first lesson in exposure, and how easily he could turn curiosity into a spectacle. And that final conversation, the one where he hurled a false accusation so vile it stole my breath, taught me what annihilation sounded like when spoken in a calm, paternal voice.

He built each moment like a courtroom demonstration: exhibit after exhibit, proving that he held the power to define me.

But the truth had a way of slipping through his rehearsed narratives.

Years later, when I finally told my sister what he'd said about Laura and that she'd supposedly called me a pedophile and didn't want me near my little brother, her eyes went wide with disbelief.

"No way that happened. I know for a fact, I promise, that isn't my mom." She stood so quickly her chair scraped the floor and flew backwards. "Wait here," she said, and before I could stop her, she called Laura into the room.

Laura came in drying her hands on a towel, still smelling faintly of dish soap and perfume. My sister looked at me. "Go ahead," she said softly, tears already gathering in her eyes. "Ask her."

My throat tightened, but I did. I repeated his words exactly, every syllable tasting like shame.

Laura froze, her face shifting from confusion to heartbreak in a single breath. "Oh, no," she said, voice trembling. "I never said that, and I would never say that about you. Never." She looked at me like I was something fragile and precious that had been dropped. "I don't know why he would tell you that."

And then she hugged me tight, shaking her head, whispering that she was sorry I'd ever heard something so awful. For the first time, I let myself believe it wasn't true. For the first time, the poison didn't take.

When she pulled back, she said quietly that this wasn't the first time it had happened. Other people; friends, even some family had come to her over the years repeating horrible things she'd supposedly said about them. Every story was different, but the source was always the same. Him.

She'd learned to recognize the pattern: the way he'd drop a cruel sentence into conversation and walk away, leaving everyone else to absorb the damage. She said she used to think it was bitterness from the divorce, punishment for leaving him. But now she understood it for what it was—an ongoing campaign to turn everyone against her, one poisoned whisper at a time.

Hearing her say that cracked something open in me. It wasn't just me he'd done this to; it was anyone who had loved or protected me. It wasn't enough for him to humiliate me. He wanted to erase every person who might keep me safe. If he could turn Laura into a villain, he could make me believe there was no harbor left. That's how isolation works—it doesn't shout, it suggests. It makes you doubt the hands reaching toward you until you stop reaching back.

For years afterward, I couldn't walk past a soccer field without feeling small again, couldn't see a folded newspaper without the twitch of panic that someone might be laughing behind it. When the word pedophile surfaced in my mind, it came not as accusation but as contamination, as if merely hearing it had stained me. That's what emotional and psychological abuse does—it hands you the weapon and convinces you it's yours.

I used to wonder why humiliation worked so well on me. Why I never fought back, never shouted. Now I understand: humiliation isn't about what happens in the moment. It's about what it teaches you to anticipate. Once shame takes root, it flowers into hypervigilance. You start scanning every room for tone, for posture, for the shift in someone's breathing that warns you another blow is coming. You learn to laugh early, to apologize before you're blamed, to vanish before the spotlight finds you.

He mistook that vanishing for maturity. He'd tell people I was "the easy one," as though compliance were a virtue. I carried that compliment for years, not realizing it was a diagnosis. Easy meant silent. Easy meant safe to ignore.

Humiliation was his favorite form of currency. It didn't just control behavior; it rewrote memory. Each new incident overwrote the last until I couldn't tell which apology belonged to which event. Eventually the shame became ambient, like background noise I didn't notice until I stepped into someone else's quiet.

There's a difference between being raised and being managed. My father managed me. Every correction was an investment in control. The less I resisted, the more convinced he became that his methods worked. By the time I was ten, he no longer needed to scold; I had internalized his voice. It lived in the pause before every decision: What will make him proud? What will make him angry? What will make him disappear again?

Even after I stopped living under his roof during visitation, the echo stayed. It followed me into classrooms, friendships, relationships. I kept mistaking tension for safety because it was the only rhythm I knew. When someone raised their voice, I felt clarity. When they were kind, I waited for the turn.

Sometimes I picture that era as a set of nested boxes: inside each one, a smaller version of myself, folded down to fit. The boy on the soccer field, the one in the kitchen with the newspaper, the one at the table trying not to cry. Each version learned to occupy less space until invisibility became a kind of skill. The irony is that invisibility is exhausting; you can't rest when your existence feels conditional.

It took me decades to understand that what he called discipline was simply domination. It wasn't about making me strong; it was about keeping me small enough that he could still feel powerful. His brand of fatherhood had nothing to do with guidance; it was theater. He wanted the audience to believe he was shaping a son, not breaking one.

And he didn't just direct that theater at me. I see it now. How he used the same script on Laura, how he whispered different lies to different people, each tailored to break the bond between them. When Laura told me later that others had come to her with terrible things she'd supposedly said about them, I saw the full picture: he'd been directing an entire cast, each of us acting out roles we didn't choose, convinced the others had turned against us.

That was his real genius; dividing the audience so no one compared notes. His stories weren't just cruel, they were strategic. He was trying to teach us not to trust one another, because united, we might have seen him clearly.

When I think of him now, I sometimes imagine him as an architect of silence. He didn't build houses; he built rooms where no one dared to speak freely. He furnished them with rules disguised as jokes and affection rationed like currency.

And he stood at the center, perfectly calm, while everyone else learned to tiptoe.

That's the genius of narcissistic control: it convinces you the architecture is love.

I see it clearly only in hindsight. The soccer field wasn't about sports. The newspaper wasn't about news. The accusation wasn't about truth. They were all demonstrations of proof that he could choose the story, and that my role in it was to agree.

People sometimes ask survivors of this kind of upbringing how they forgave. I didn't. Forgiveness implies an apology, or at least recognition, and there has never been either. What I have instead is understanding: the recognition that he operated within the limits of his own emptiness. Understanding is colder than forgiveness but more honest. It lets me name the damage without carrying it.

There are days when the old reflexes still show up. When someone says "we need to talk," my chest tightens. When a group laughs too loud, my body braces for the target to be me. But those reactions no longer own me; they're just echoes.

If I could speak to that boy now, the one crying on the soccer field, the one shrinking beside the kitchen counter, the one too scared to tell his mother what was said about him—I'd tell him this: again, none of it was your fault. You were a child trying to survive an adult's insecurity. You thought you were broken because he told you so. But you weren't broken; you were adapting. Survival isn't weakness. It's proof of life.

The hardest part of healing has been unlearning the idea that safety comes from silence. Silence kept me alive then, but it kept me small afterward. Speaking, even now, feels like defiance. Every sentence is a door cracked open, letting light into a place he wanted to keep dark.

Writing this chapter has been that light. It's the sound of my own voice, steady and unfiltered, saying what should have been said decades ago: you can stop performing. You can stop apologizing. You can stop mistaking fear for respect.

He tried to build a son out of obedience and shame.

What he made instead was a witness.

And the witness, finally, has learned to speak.

Reader's Note

If your chest feels tight right now, that's okay.

Writing this chapter felt the same way to me.

The scenes you just read aren't places I visit often. They live at the edge of who I was—small, confused, desperate to be good when good was never the goal. For years I carried them in silence, believing they proved something was wrong with me.

They didn't. They proved something was wrong with him.

If you've ever been humiliated for simply existing, please know that shame was never yours to hold. The cruelty that shaped us was a reflection of their fear, not our worth.

I used to think survival meant pretending it never happened. Now I know survival means telling it anyway, and giving the story a safer ending than the one we lived.

Before you turn the page, take a breath. Stretch. Drink water. Look at something living.

What comes next is how control changes shape; how generosity can hide a leash, and how, little by little, I began to cut it.

And if you need to hear it: I'm okay. Not because the past vanished, but because I've learned how to live alongside it. Healing isn't a straight line from broken to fixed; it's a series of small, stubborn recoveries. Some days are hard. Most days, I am not defined by the shame I was taught to carry. For the last decade, I hadn't really thought about these memories often. Maybe that's what healing actually is—the day a wound becomes only a story.

Chapter 7 – The Price of Help

My dad learned to buy silence the way some men learn to buy suits: with a practiced hand and an eye for how it would look in public.

I was about twenty-four and trying to finish college without promising my life to anyone when he called in that tone that made favors sound like duties. "I need to meet you in town after your classes," he said. "Right by where you work. Pick a time that's easy for you. I just need you to sign something."

He wouldn't explain more than that. "I can't talk right now, but this would be a huge help for me." The phrasing was familiar. Every "help" of his came wrapped in moral obligation, an invisible ledger where I always owed more than I received.

We met two blocks from my job, by the bank on the corner. There was a permanent trash can there with a flat metal top where people balanced briefcases or checked their phones. The sky was gray, the kind of afternoon that felt like waiting.

He arrived with another man I didn't know; both of them were quiet and businesslike. My father carried a slim leather briefcase, the kind he always used for effect, even when he didn't need it. He pulled a personal check from inside, set it face down on that flat metal lid, and handed me a pen.

At first, I thought it was paperwork. He told me to endorse the back. When I asked what I was signing, he flipped the check over and said, "See? Just a check." My name was on the payee line.

My eyes dropped to the amount: one hundred and thirty thousand dollars. The number still sounds obscene in my head.

"Wait, if I sign this, could it affect my taxes or anything?" I asked, trying to sound practical in a moment that felt anything but. My heart was hammering; my palms were slick. A part of me already knew something was off, since there was no reason for him to involve me in anything worth that much money. Maybe because we didn't share the same last name.

The other man stayed silent. My father's voice tightened. "Well, I guess you could sign it and take it and it would all be yours if you were that kind of person," he said, part test, part reproach.

There it was again: the bait of generosity, hooked with guilt.

I signed. I was tired of doors that stayed closed and options that came with strings I didn't want to read. We shook hands. I walked to my car. They walked into the bank together. That is what I saw.

The next few days blurred together. I kept checking my bank account, just checking to make sure nothing was happening there. I don't know who issued the check or why my name was on the payee line; I don't know the details of what happened after I walked away. All I can report is what I experienced: my name on the payee line, my signature on the back, and the absence of any direct benefit to me afterward.

Later, when I replayed that day, I realized what had unsettled me most wasn't the check I endorsed—it was the missing clarity. He'd managed to turn trust into participation, silence into complicity. The exact same skill he'd honed for years, making control look like cooperation. But now had a dollar sign attached.

It took me years to understand that what happened wasn't really about money. It was about leverage. About seeing how much of my autonomy I was willing to trade for peace.

The lesson I carried forward was simple and practical: not all help is neutral. After that day, I learned to look for terms and consequences—who benefits, who pays the price, and how much of my own freedom is assumed in the exchange.

Chapter 8 – The Last Goodnight

The night before was so normal it almost feels made up now.

Mom got home from work around the usual time, still in her office clothes: black slacks, a cream blouse, her work shoes clicking softly across the kitchen tile. She dropped her purse on the counter like she always did, sighed the same long sigh she did after every workday, and went straight to the kitchen to start dinner. The sound of cabinet doors opening and closing, the clatter of pans, the faint hum of the stove fan; those were the sounds of home.

I don't even remember what she cooked that night, just that the house smelled warm and familiar, like comfort had a scent. It was the same smell that used to cling to her sweaters in winter: butter, detergent, and a hint of something floral from her perfume. While she stirred dinner, she mentioned that the news was calling for a snowstorm later that week, Thursday or Friday, maybe even a blizzard if the system grew large enough.

She hated driving in snow and was already hoping her office would close if it got bad. Still, she talked about it with a small smile, like the idea of an unexpected day off sounded nice; a tiny reprieve from the endless rhythm of work and bills.

While she stirred, she started talking about the stores she wanted to visit that weekend, and how she was finally going to find the perfect piece of furniture for the living room, something that would fit near the entryway and tie everything together. She'd been saying that for months, always scanning stores and scrolling through websites for inspiration.

Later that night she called me into the office to show me
what she'd found. She had printouts spread across the desk;
photos of tables and cabinets, handwritten notes in the
margins with pen circles around her favorites. She was so
proud of how the house was coming together. It was twice as
big as the townhouse and somewhat fancy, and it was hers.
After years of making do, of doing without, she'd built a
space that reflected her: warm, practical, welcoming.

After dinner, we watched TV together for a while. She
stretched out in the recliner part of the couch with her legs
up, a blanket over her knees. She mentioned her back had
been sore again and that she'd made an appointment with the
chiropractor for later that week. Then she said her legs hurt;
just in passing, like it was one of those small physical
annoyances everyone collects in adulthood. The TV flickered
across the room, the light shifting gently over her face, over
the walls, over everything ordinary. It was a quiet evening, the
kind that never feels remarkable until it becomes the last one.

When I got up to head upstairs, I said, "I'm going to bed.
Love you!"

She smiled and said, "Goodnight, love you."

I didn't know those would be the last words we'd ever say to
each other.

It was a normal Tuesday in early 2009, the kind of winter
morning that doesn't give you any warning.

We'd only been in the new house about eight months. Mom
had just sold the townhouse we grew up in, using the money
to buy this 55-plus home she loved. It was quiet, light-filled,
perfectly hers. Everything was on one floor except for my

space upstairs, a bedroom, bathroom, and a large finished storage room that I used for exercise equipment and overflow from a life still in motion. I was planning to stay about a year, save up, and then buy a place of my own. It was supposed to be a temporary chapter for both of us. Her starting fresh in a house she'd finally earned, and me in my twenties, getting ready for whatever came next.

My alarm went off to wake me. The house was still dark and held that deep winter silence that almost hums. I rolled out of bed, half awake, and padded toward the bathroom. The carpet was cool under my feet. As I crossed the room, another sound threaded through the quiet; faint, repetitive, mechanical. Her alarm clock.

It came from downstairs, sharp and steady beneath the whisper of the heater, those quick electronic beeps that never matched the calm of our mornings. She usually woke up before me to make coffee and start her routine. So, I figured she must've hit snooze. Nothing unusual.

I showered, got dressed, and checked my phone. The alarm was still going when I came down the stairs. Each step made it louder, more insistent, echoing up through the stairwell.

The kitchen light was still off. The air smelled faintly like last night's dinner and her vanilla plug-in air freshener. I turned on the coffee maker, the one she swore made it "just right," and waited for the familiar click and gurgle. The sound didn't come. I realized I hadn't added water. My hands were clumsy, distracted by that continuing beep from down the hall.

I walked through the dining room toward her bedroom.

"Mom?" I called softly. "Mom, you up?"

Her room was dark except for the night-light's small amber glow across the room. I could see her outline under the covers, lying on her left side like she always did, shoulder slightly hunched, blanket pulled high.

I crossed to the alarm clock first, turned it off, and said her name again.

"Mom. Mom, you have to get up now."

She didn't move.

For a second, I just stood there. The quiet that followed the silenced alarm was heavy, unnatural. My ears rang in the stillness. I walked back around the foot of the bed, over to the doorway and flipped on the overhead light.

Her hair spilled from under the blanket, messy in the way it always was in the morning. She was tucked in tight.

Something in me already knew.

I pulled the covers back and froze. Her skin was gray on top, purple underneath where her face met the pillow. Her lips were slightly parted, her expression peaceful in a way that made it worse.

I said her name again and again, each time louder until the sound tore at my throat. I grabbed her arm—it was cold, heavy, the stiffness resisting me. The only warmth left was near her hip where the blanket had trapped it.

The room smelled like fabric softener and her night cream. The clock still showed 6:47. The heater clicked on. The ordinary sounds kept happening, but none of them belonged anymore.

I knew what I was looking at.

And I knew it was too late.

I called 911.

My voice didn't sound like mine. It was high, tight, echoing back at me through the phone speaker as if someone else were speaking through my mouth. I told the dispatcher that my mother wasn't breathing; that she had passed away.

The woman on the line asked me to start CPR.

I said, "She's already cold and stiff."

She didn't seem to hear me. "Move her out of the bed and onto the floor," she instructed, firm and professional. "CPR will be more effective that way."

I said, "I can't."

The next thing she said carved itself into my memory. Her voice rose, sharp with frustration.

"Don't you even want to try saving your mom?"

The words hit like a slap. I still hear them sometimes, even now, in quiet rooms.

I started shaking. Then her tone softened. She told me the ambulance was less than a minute away and that they could help her.

When the call disconnected after the first police officer pulled into the driveway, the silence in the house came roaring back.

The police arrived first—a sudden knock, then the creak of the storm door. They stepped inside, scanning the space automatically, hands on their radios. They moved quickly, voices low, calm but alert. I pointed to the bedroom. Then the ambulance screamed past the house, siren still blaring. I bolted outside, waving my arms, yelling that they'd missed the driveway. My breath hung in white clouds in the January air.

They reversed down the street, tires crunching over the thin frost, and rushed up the sidewalk carrying their machines and bags. I stepped aside as they passed through the front door. Their boots thudded on the hardwood, the zippers of their gear rasping open like Velcro tearing.

I stayed in the living room. I couldn't make myself go back to the bedroom. I already knew from before calling 911. The sound of voices; short, efficient commands—filtered through the hallway. Then came the silence that means everything is over.

I called my Nana, only three minutes away, and said the vaguest thing imaginable: "Can you come to the house? Something's wrong with Mom." My voice cracked on wrong. I couldn't make myself say the rest.

She arrived in record time. I heard her car door slam, the quick rhythm of her shoes on the porch. When she saw my face, she knew before I said anything. She went straight into the room while I stood frozen in the living room doorway, staring at nothing.

When she came back out, her face was pale, her jaw trembling. For once, she didn't say "we don't cry in front of people" the way she always did when things got hard. She just wrapped her arms around me and guided me toward the kitchen, gently steering me away from the bedroom door.

Her voice was steady when she told me, "You have to be strong now."

I knew what that meant—don't fall apart. So, I didn't. I was used to keeping it together, to holding my face still during chaos.

She told me to call my office and let them know I wouldn't be in. Then she said to call my father. The words felt mechanical, like reading off a checklist.

I ended up emailing my manager instead, just a short message: I won't be coming in today. My mom passed away this morning. The reply came almost immediately, kind and gentle, telling me to take as much time as I needed. I stared at the screen, rereading the words as if they could make any of it make sense.

After that, I called my father. I don't remember a single word of that conversation, even though I remember almost everything else about that day. The sound of his voice is blank in my mind, like static that erased itself.

A few minutes later, the EMTs came out. One of them, a woman with long brown hair, walked up to me slowly. Her gloves were still on. She rested one hand on my arm and said, softly, "There was absolutely nothing you could have done to change the outcome. I'm so sorry for your loss."

Her eyes were kind. And I really appreciate her confirming that with me. But, I still wonder if the 911 operator had told the EMTs that I hadn't tried to save her, as instructed.

Then they packed up their gear. The click of their cases closing was louder than it should have been. The siren stayed off as they pulled away.

The police said the coroner was on the way. It would be about an hour. Everyone stayed—Nana, my uncle and aunt who arrived during the chaos. Nobody wanted to leave her, or me, alone. The house felt smaller than it ever had before, the air too still, as if even the walls understood that something vital had stopped.

When the coroner arrived, I moved into the kitchen.

I couldn't bear for my last memory of her to be a black bag on a stretcher, lifted into that black Dodge truck with the cab over the bed. I knew exactly where they'd park; the right side of the driveway, and I knew that once the door opened, I'd never see her again. From where I stood, I could still hear everything: the slow shuffle of shoes on the hardwood, the zip of the bag, the soft murmur of professionals trying not to echo in a house that was already too quiet.

I pressed both hands flat against the counter, staring at the veins in the marble. The surface was cold beneath my palms. The smell of coffee that had gone cold hung in the air, bitter and sweet. My work laptop still sat open from that morning, its blue glow spilling across the countertop. New email notifications kept appearing one after another; small pings announcing condolences from coworkers who had already heard, offering sympathy and saying they'd be at the funeral. Each ping felt both distant and tender, like the world was trying to reach me through fog I couldn't yet see out of.

When the coroner wheeled the stretcher out, I stayed in the kitchen, pretending to check my phone, pretending to breathe normally. The front door opened. I felt the cold air rush down the hallway, the metallic creak of the gurney wheels bumping over the threshold. I didn't look. I didn't need to. The sound was enough to etch itself in memory.

When the door closed, the house fell silent again, the kind of silence that has shape and weight.

An hour later, there was a knock.

My father.

He said, "I'm sorry, Jeff," from the doorway and opened his arms for a hug. It startled me; he never apologized, never said words like that, nor did we ever hug. I took a few steps forward and hugged him back, more out of confusion than comfort. His jacket was cold. He smelled like tea and winter air.

Then, as always, he took control.

"Get a notepad," he said, walking straight past me into the living room. His voice had already shifted from soft to directive. We sat at the table and began making lists: calls to make, funeral homes to contact, things to do. He was calm, detached, almost businesslike. That was his way of surviving; control as oxygen.

I followed, because there was nothing else to do. My handwriting looked foreign on the page, letters slanting unevenly, as if even my hands were disoriented. He dictated names and numbers while I wrote them down. Somewhere behind us, Nana was still on the phone with relatives, her voice trembling every time she said passed away.

Someone ordered lunch; hoagies and sides. I couldn't eat. The smell of onions and vinegar turned my stomach, but people kept urging me to have a bite, as if chewing might make the day seem normal again. I finally took half a sandwich, not tasting it, just swallowing for the sake of others. They looked relieved.

I remember staring at the plate afterward, the crusts still there, and thinking how strange it was that eating could make anyone happy when someone had just died in the next room.

That was the morning everything changed.

The house stayed the same shape, the same walls, the same furniture. But without her in it, it was just an echo. Empty.

That first night, after everyone left, I walked from room to room turning off lights I didn't remember turning on. The house felt too bright, like it hadn't yet learned she was gone. Every switch I flipped left another room behind, swallowed by dark. The hum of the refrigerator, the faint tick of the clock in the hallway; every small sound felt louder than it ever had before.

I remember standing at the bottom of the stairs, looking up toward my room, and realizing the only other heartbeat in the house was gone. The silence had mass; it pressed against my chest like gravity. I couldn't make myself go upstairs. I slept on the couch for the next few nights, TV flickering low just so the air would have something to move against. I told myself it was to listen for the phone in case someone called, but really, I just couldn't bear the sound of the house breathing without her.

When I finally started sleeping in my room again, a few days later, the first thing I did was go into her bedroom. The air still smelled faintly like her—lavender lotion and the powder she kept on her dresser. The bed looked exactly as it had that morning, the blanket folded halfway down, the pillow dented in the shape of her head.

The alarm clock was still there. The same one that kept beeping that morning—the sound that still lives in my head to this day. I unplugged it from the wall and threw it straight into the trash. I didn't ever want to risk hearing it again.

A few sterile white wrappers and EKG pads from the EMTs were still scattered on the floor beside the bed. I picked them up one by one and threw them away too, needing the room to feel like hers again. The trash can filled with silence.

Then I closed her bedroom door and kept it closed. She never slept with it closed—never—but I couldn't stand to see it open. Closing it was the only way I could let her rest, and the only way I could stop pretending she might still come out.

For a while, I kept glancing toward that door anyway. Part of me kept expecting to hear her slippers against the floor, her voice calling my name, the coffee starting in the kitchen. The mind is cruel that way; it doesn't accept reality all at once. It lets you believe for a few seconds at a time that the world hasn't changed.

It was a goodbye from someone who wasn't ready, but had to do it anyway.

My mom was gone. The person I called whenever I needed to vent about my father, the one who still protected me even when I was grown. She was tough, sharp-tongued when she needed to be, never afraid to yell or tell someone off if they deserved it. She was my safety net, my compass, my living proof that the things I remembered weren't just exaggerations of a kid's imagination.

Losing her wasn't just losing my mom. It was losing my buffer, my witness, my validator, the one person who understood how to stand up to him even when she couldn't always win. Without her, my version of the story suddenly had no corroboration. The truth still existed, but now it was trapped inside me.

Within the next few days and weeks, something strange happened. My father started calling more; checking in like he finally cared. For a while, I wanted to believe it. I wanted to think maybe her death had cracked something open in him, that grief had made him human again.

It actually felt comforting at first, like maybe losing her had forced him to see what really mattered. He'd ask about my classes, about whether I was eating enough, about whether I needed help paying bills. He sounded like the kind of dad people wish they had.

But underneath, something still felt off. His voice carried that old weight again; too patient, too careful, like someone waiting for you to relax before springing a trap. I couldn't name it then, but I knew it. It was the sound of control, polished into concern.

Deep down, I knew better, and my intuition didn't let me down this time either. You learn to read a man like that without realizing it: his breathing, his pauses, the shape of his silence. I knew that whatever this new kindness was, it came with a price I hadn't been told yet.

That winter, the house and I both learned what absence really meant. The walls held their shape, but the warmth had gone out of them. Every time I walked past her closed door, it felt like walking past a chapter that hadn't ended cleanly.

She was gone.

And for the first time, I understood that grief isn't the same as pain.

Pain eventually dulls.

Grief just changes rooms.

Chapter 9 – The Will

Funerals are supposed to be about closure, but what I remember most is exhaustion.

Everything about that week felt like moving underwater; each motion heavy, muffled, delayed. The days blurred together into errands and phone calls, into the sound of my name being spoken in other people's voices. I remember standing outside the funeral home that morning, the sky the same flat gray as the parking lot, snow packed along the curb from the storm the day before. When the doors opened, the first thing that hit me was the smell: hydrangea and cold winter air, mixed with perfume, wool coats, and grief.

The room was already full. Some of my father's side of the family filed in, their voices hushed but constant, like background static. Even Uncle Ray was there, sitting toward the back with another uncle, in case he made a scene. I felt like an intruder at my own mother's service, surrounded by faces that all had opinions about her but none who really knew her.

When the service began, I took a seat in front near the aisle and tried to disappear into the hum of quiet sobs. My Uncle Sam, my mom's brother-in-law, stood at the lectern and read the eulogy I had written. Public speaking has never been my thing. I wanted the words to be hers and mine, not something I stammered through while shaking. Hearing Uncle Sam read them made it sound like a prayer instead of a performance.

His voice broke halfway through the last paragraph, the one about how she could make a house feel like home even when she was barely keeping herself upright. The sound cracked the air, and suddenly everyone was crying. The room filled with that soft, endless sound of shared loss—like rain hitting glass.

Afterward, a line formed in front of the casket: friends, coworkers, cousins, neighbors, each taking a turn to cry on my shoulder. I remember comforting them, telling them it would be okay, that she had lived a good life. It felt like my job to keep them standing. Their tears soaked into my suit jacket until the fabric clung cold to my skin. People I hadn't seen in years promised I could call if I ever needed anything. I nodded and smiled, knowing that once the casseroles cooled and the flowers wilted, those offers would fade like the scent of lilies after the door closes.

I barely remember the drive to the cemetery. The snowstorm that mom was worried about had hit the day before, leaving the world covered in white quiet. The windshield wipers scraped against ice; the defroster blew air that smelled like antifreeze. The only detail that remains clear is my car slipping on the icy hill that led up to the burial site. For a second, the tires spun, the whole car shuddered, and I thought how fitting it was to lose control even there. Then we were at the top, and the world turned silent again. I don't remember much else after that. I don't have any memories of the actual burial or anything that happened there, except placing a flower on top of her casket and the funeral director removing the decorative items from the casket and giving them to me. To be kept as a keepsake.

The luncheon afterward was for anyone who wanted to come. The room smelled like coffee and sympathy. I tried to play with the little kids, to keep the noise light. My mom's brothers were kind; they pressed folded bills into my hand to help cover the cost of the luncheon. Their kindness hit me harder than all the hugs at the church.

When it was time to pay, I went into the kitchen. The total was written on a small notepad with the caterer's name across the top. I left what I thought was right, and rounded up to add a tip, but my brain was still fogged from the day, and my sense of proportion warped by grief and fatigue.

The next morning, my Nana called to check on me. Her voice carried that steady, no-nonsense comfort she always had. After asking if I'd eaten and slept, she mentioned she had stopped by the caterer's office to "take care of the tip."

"I know you did what you thought was fine," she said gently, "but I wanted to make sure they were thanked properly."

It wasn't criticism, just another example of her quiet way of fixing what grief makes messy. I thanked her, embarrassed that she'd had to do it, grateful she had anyway.

After we hung up, I sat at the kitchen table, staring at the notepad where I'd made my list of funeral calls. The ink had smudged from the condensation on a glass of water. For the first time all week, I felt the ache settle in; the kind that has no single source. Grief is strange that way. It doesn't always announce itself with tears. Sometimes it just waits, quiet and patient, until the house goes still again.

In the days that followed, grief took on a bureaucratic shape; calls, forms, signatures. My mother's death was becoming a checklist.

The strangest problem turned out to be her car. It sat neatly in the garage, spotless as always, tank full, right next to my car. She had filled it the prior weekend after hearing about the snowstorm. Even in her last days, she was planning ahead, making sure everything was ready.

The car was a 2007 Acura, still gleaming under the fluorescent light. The air inside smelled faintly like leather and her. Every surface was immaculate. Her spare pair of gloves rested on the passenger seat, palms together, fingers straight. It felt like the last part of her routine still in motion.

I drove it a few times that week, short trips to the office and back, the radio still tuned to her favorite radio station. The songs sounded too bright, too alive for the silence that followed. It felt like borrowing a piece of her, as though she might climb in beside me at the next stoplight.

But reality crept in: even though the lease payments were current through the end of the month and a week into the next month, the car wasn't mine.

I called the financing company to ask what to do. The hold music was soft piano, looping endlessly while I waited for someone to answer. When a woman finally picked up, I explained everything as calmly as I could. She didn't want to talk to me. I wasn't on the account. The policy was clear: "We can't discuss this with you."

When I told her the owner had passed away, her voice softened just slightly. "I'm so sorry for your loss," she said, as if it were a script. Then: "As long as the payments are current, you could continue paying them."

Continue them. As if that was a solution.

I didn't need two cars. And I didn't want one that carried her ghost.

After a few more calls that led nowhere, each one ending in the same polite wall of policy, I decided to handle it in person. I didn't want a repo truck coming around the house. So, I drove her car to the local dealership, Honda, the sister brand to her Acura. I parked it under the dealership sign, the way she used to park perfectly between the lines, never crooked, never rushed.

Before going inside, I sat there for a minute with my hands on the steering wheel. The heater hummed. The keys were warm in my palm, and I realized they were the last thing she had touched every day before leaving the house.

I took a few photos inside and out—proof that the car was spotless, that I'd done what I could to prevent a repossession from looking like neglect. I also snapped a picture of the car under the sign, exactly as I parked it, showing the moment before turning it in.

Inside, I explained the situation. The manager listened, nodding, but his eyes drifted toward his computer screen halfway through my story. When I finished, he looked at me like I was speaking another language.

"Sorry," he said finally, "there's nothing we can do."

I told him I didn't know what else to do, that it wasn't my car, that the owner was gone, and that someone needed to take responsibility. He repeated himself: "We can't help you."

So I set both sets of keys on the corner of his desk and said, "Okay. Then I'll walk home."

He blinked, unsure what to do next.

I paused at the doorway, turned back, and asked, "I forgot about the license plate. Do you have a screwdriver I could borrow?"

He said, "That is our plate and stays with the car."

That was the only part he wanted to claim. But if he claimed the plate, he claimed the car it was attached to.

Outside, the air bit at my lungs as I started walking. The afternoon winter sky was clear, but the kind that makes everything else look gray. My shoes crunched over the salted sidewalk. Cars passed by, with short bursts of wind hitting my back as they passed.

Halfway home, I looked back once, but the dealership had already vanished behind the bend. I contemplated driving by later that week to see if the car was still there, but I never did, because I really didn't want to know.

It felt like I had handed off the last physical piece of her I could touch.

For years she'd worked so hard to afford that car; to have something nice that was hers, dependable, clean, and perfect in a way the rest of life rarely was. And now, I'd left it behind with strangers who couldn't even say her name.

Grief, I was learning, doesn't just take people. It takes rituals. It takes the things they built, the objects that carried their fingerprints. One by one, it strips away the evidence that they were ever here.

That day, walking home through the chill of winter, I realized that loss isn't always loud. Sometimes it's just the quiet sound of keys hitting a desk—and the long walk after, when you have to teach yourself to let go of what's already gone.

The weeks after the funeral blurred into paperwork and logistics. Grief became administrative.

Every day brought new envelopes; creditor notices, insurance forms, legal documents stamped with words like estate and executor. Each one arrived with the same formal condolences and instructions: sign here, submit this, attach a death certificate. I kept a stack of manila folders on the dining room table, the same place where she used to set out dinner. It was surreal—where she once placed napkins, I now placed documents proving she was gone.

My father helped me sort through them over the phone, his tone professional, detached, as if I were one of his clients. "It's routine," he'd say. "Don't overthink it." We went to the courthouse together once to file paperwork. I can't remember what exactly it was for. Maybe probate or prothonotary, but I remember the way the clerk's office smelled faintly of toner and old carpet. I remember him standing beside me at the counter, confident, practiced, explaining everything before I could even form a question.

It required a notice to be placed in a legal publication; something about creditors having a chance to come forward. The clerk told us the cost. It was a couple hundred dollars. He pulled out his wallet and paid without a second thought, like paying a parking ticket.

I ordered estate checks. We followed every rule. When you have a lawyer for a father, there's no other way.

At first, I was grateful for his help. I told myself it was his version of showing up. It made things easier, or at least, it looked that way. But after a while, I started to feel the shift. Every signature, every form, every visit to the courthouse became another opportunity for him to oversee. To monitor. To insert himself into the process.

Control doesn't always look like shouting. Sometimes it looks like guidance so tight you forget it's a leash. Sometimes it looks like assistance that never lets you breathe on your own.

Once the paperwork was moving, I turned my focus to the house. Selling it felt like the only option.

The plan to buy my own place was still there, but this house, the quiet 55-plus community, the neighbors who waved politely from their driveways, felt wrong now. They all would stop outside if they saw me and told me that they would love if I decided to stay in that house. But the master bedroom was a wound I couldn't live beside. Every time I passed the doorway, I felt the echo of that morning; the alarm, the stillness, the impossible quiet. I couldn't imagine sleeping in the same room where I found her and pretending it could ever be mine.

So, I started cleaning.

The first few days were practical: clothes for donation, photo frames wrapped in newspaper, boxes labeled keep or storage. But when I reached her dresser, everything slowed.

There was a small box on top, the one she kept her most important papers in. I remembered seeing her take it out sometimes, thumbing through bills and warranty cards, muttering about receipts. It was the kind of box no one else would ever think twice about, but I knew it mattered.

Inside, beneath a stack of folded papers, was a thick envelope with three notarized copies of her will.

Each one had an embossed seal pressed so deeply you could feel it under your fingertips. I ran my thumb over the raised circle, tracing the edge like it might explain something.

I opened one. Her handwriting was on the signature line, steady and deliberate. Every asset, account, and belonging, everything, was left to me.

For a few seconds, I just stared at the page. I could picture her sitting somewhere at a notary's desk, patient and precise, making sure it was done right. She had planned for this moment long before either of us was ready for it. It was her way of protecting me one last time.

Then I called my father.

"I found my mom's will," I said. "It's notarized. All three copies have seals on them."

There was a pause—too long. The kind of pause where you can hear someone thinking, recalibrating. Then his voice came through, colder than before.

"Well," he said, "I guess it's all yours. Everything is yours."

I was shocked. The tone wasn't pride or comfort. It was sharp, almost disgusted, as if I'd taken something from him.

I didn't know what to say, so I said nothing.

The silence between us stretched. For a moment, I thought the call had dropped. Then I realized he was still there, breathing, waiting, but the conversation was already over.

In that silence, something small but unmistakable shifted.

For the first time, I heard it clearly; the sound of his composure cracking. For a man who prided himself on control, with every word and every gesture measured, he had let a piece of truth slip through. It was fleeting, but real: he wasn't mourning her. He was mourning the loss of control.

He caught himself quickly, changed the subject, moved on to some procedural detail about the estate. But the damage was done.

I remember setting the phone down on the counter afterward and staring at the will still open in front of me. The page looked heavy with meaning. It wasn't about the money. It was about the message she left behind: I trust you more than anyone else. I want you to have peace when I'm gone.

That was the moment I realized she had outsmarted him one last time. She hadn't fought him in life—she'd simply written her truth in ink, sealed and notarized, where he couldn't twist it.

And for the first time since she died, I felt something that wasn't grief.

It was gratitude.

Later, I was back in the master bedroom cleaning and gathering donations. The house was quiet; too quiet. The kind of quiet that hums in your ears after a storm. It was just me, the faint whir of the heater, and the soft shuffle of cardboard boxes being filled and taped shut.

I went back to the box on her dresser. The one that had held the will, the small archive of her carefulness. The envelopes at the bottom were older envelopes. Postmarks faded, edges soft, and ink smudged where years of fingertips had brushed over them. I started opening them, one by one.

Most were letters from her attorney, formal, impersonal, typed on letterhead that had browned slightly with age. Custody records. Visitation schedules. Words like petition and affidavit. The vocabulary of survival. These were the documents of years she'd spent fighting for the right to raise me without interference. Seeing her handwriting in the margins: small notes, underlines, a checkmark here and there was like hearing her whisper across time, still trying to protect me from him.

Then came envelopes addressed in a handwriting I recognized immediately. My father's. His penmanship was as distinct as his voice: bold, certain, impatient. The same pressure in every stroke, like he couldn't even write without performing authority.

I hesitated. For a second, I almost put them back, still sealed. But they were mine now; legally part of the estate, and, in a way, part of her.

So I opened them.

Each one was a performance in ink. The sentences were perfectly balanced, the tone precise and manipulative. Lectures disguised as logic. Apologies that shifted blame halfway through. Flattery undercut by threat. It was the same voice I knew from phone calls, dinners, arguments, but now preserved forever on paper.

Reading them felt invasive, but I couldn't stop. It was like watching him rehearse cruelty in slow motion. The cadence was unmistakable. You could almost hear him pausing for effect, even in silence.

And then I found another envelope, different from the rest.

It was thinner, its flap resealed with old tape that had yellowed around the edges. The return address belonged to her attorney. Inside were two folded papers: a letter and a document with official markings.

I unfolded the top sheet. It was short, just a note confirming that enclosed were the results he had requested.

The second paper was heavier, crisp. A paternity test.

At the top, it said the test had been requested by my father, as his own legal representative. The date was decades old. The results were printed neatly in a small box at the bottom. 99.99% probability of paternity.

Even now, those numbers hum in my head like an insult disguised as science.

He had gone to a lab to confirm what everyone already knew; to search for proof of blood in the absence of love. It wasn't about doubt; it was about ownership. Proof that I belonged to him on paper, even if he'd never earned the title in practice.

I sat on the edge of her bed for a long time, the paper trembling in my hands. The heater clicked on again, breaking the silence.

I placed the documents back carefully, like they were radioactive, something that could still burn even after all these years.

Then, deeper in the stack, I found older papers. Documents from her first marriage, legal correspondence written on onion-skin paper, her maiden name looping in the elegant cursive she'd abandoned after remarrying. Her life before him. Before me.

I kept going until I reached the very bottom, where the papers had yellowed and curled at the corners. The box was no longer just a container; it was a timeline. A record of everything she had survived before I ever learned what survival meant.

I sat there surrounded by her history, realizing that even in death, she was still telling me the truth. Just not in words.

Then I found something else.

There, beneath our Social Security cards and birth certificates, was one last envelope. It was thinner than the rest, yellowed around the edges, the flap sealed but no longer tight. The paper was fragile; soft from being handled too many times, as if someone had opened it, read it, and then folded it back again and again, trying to forget.

My mother's name and address were written on the front in my father's unmistakable handwriting; the kind that always looked like a command, even when it wasn't. Every letter slanted forward, like it was pushing through the page.

I hesitated before opening it. My hands felt too heavy. The air in the room seemed to thicken, the hum of the heater suddenly too loud. I told myself it was just another letter, or more legal talk, more arguments. But something about it felt different. The envelope felt alive, pulsing with the weight of something waiting to be revealed.

Inside was a single sheet of lined yellow paper, folded in thirds. The handwriting was larger this time, more personal, less rehearsed. I could almost see the speed of it; ink darker where the pen had pressed too hard, lighter where it raced.

I unfolded it and began to read.

It wasn't a letter.

It was a verdict.

In deliberate, calculated lines of blue ink, he built his case for why my mother should end her pregnancy. Why she should end me.

The word abortion appeared halfway down the page, as if to make it clear this wasn't suggestion but instruction. Seeing it there, written in the same hand that once signed my child support checks, felt like being punched in the chest.

The language around it was polished, almost soothing in places, the way people soften their voices when they're saying something unspeakable. He'd written it like a closing argument, full of logic and false compassion. Phrases like it's the sensible thing to do and you're not ready lined up neatly beside words about timing and money and reputation. It was pity dressed as reason.

There was no pleading, no emotion. Just a blueprint for erasure.

At the bottom, in his careful, practiced hand, he'd signed only his shortened first name. No closing, no sincerely, no yours truly, nothing human. Just his name, beneath a plea for my nonexistence.

I froze.

My eyes scanned the page again, desperate to find another meaning. To convince myself I was misreading it, that maybe it was a hypothetical, a draft, a misunderstanding. But there it was. Plain. Unflinching. Final.

He hadn't wanted me.

Not later, when I disappointed him.

Not when I grew up too quiet, or too sensitive, or too much like her.

From the very beginning.

The realization moved through me slowly, like ice melting through veins. My throat went dry. I could feel my pulse in my ears. I kept staring at his signature, the same familiar loops and angles I'd once practiced as a kid when I tried to mimic his handwriting. It hit me that I had spent years trying to earn the approval of a man who, before I even took my first breath, had tried to argue me out of existence.

I sat down hard on the edge of the bed. The paper trembled in my hands, but the words stayed still, heavy and permanent.

Everything I thought I understood about our story bent under the weight of that single sheet of paper. Every memory of his coldness, every withheld compliment, every test of obedience; they all made sense now.

It wasn't that I had failed him.

It was that my very existence had always been the failure.

The sound of the furnace kicked on again, startling me. It blew warm air across the room, but I couldn't feel any of it. I folded the paper carefully, like it was something sacred or cursed, and slid it back into the envelope.

That letter didn't just reveal something about him. It revealed the original wound. The first betrayal, written before I had a name.

It was the kind of discovery that doesn't end a story, it rewrites the beginning.

I didn't tell anyone right away. The envelope went back into the box, but the words stayed echoing through every quiet minute of the next few days. I'd go about my routine of work, laundry, dishes, mail, and still hear that single word in my head like a distant siren: abortion.

It followed me through the house like a presence, invisible but constant. Every time I passed her dresser, I could feel the weight of that letter pressing from inside the box, like it was humming at a frequency only I could hear.

Finally, a few days later, I couldn't hold it anymore. I picked up the phone and called Nana.

The line rang twice before she answered, always on the second ring, always with that familiar blend of strength and warmth. I told her I'd been cleaning the house, going through old papers, and that I'd found something unexpected. She said softly, "What kind of something?"

I hesitated. Even saying it out loud felt like crossing a line. "It was a letter from my dad," I said finally. "He told Mom to... to have an abortion"

The silence that followed was so complete it startled me. I thought maybe the call had dropped—her old wall phone sometimes cut out when it rained—but then I heard her breathing.

She wasn't speechless because she didn't believe me.

She was speechless because she did.

When she finally spoke, her voice quivered—fragile, unsteady, like something inside her was giving way.

Between breaths she said, "I always wondered where your mother got that idea in her head. I always wondered what made her think about an abortion." Her words came haltingly, as though she was piecing together memories in real time. "I remember her telling me once, just once, that she didn't know what to do back then and that there was pressure, but she wouldn't say from who. I thought she meant herself. I thought she was scared. But now..."

Her voice trailed off, thin and shaking. "Now I know. It was *that* man. I am floored."

The sound of her quietly sniffling was quiet but raw, like grief that had waited decades for a reason to surface.

Hearing her say it out loud made the whole thing heavier. It wasn't just my discovery anymore; it was a wound re-opened across generations.

For a long moment, neither of us spoke. I could hear the tick of her grandfather clock through the receiver—the same one that stood near the wall phone in the family room. The second hand kept moving, steady and relentless, as if time refused to pause for what we'd just learned.

"I'm so sorry you had to find that," she whispered finally. "But I'm glad you did. She carried that truth alone for so long. Maybe it's time someone else knew."

Her words settled in my chest like a stone and a blessing at once.

When we hung up, I sat on the floor beside the dresser, the phone still in my hand. The silence in the house was different now; not empty, but aware. I realized that in a way, my mother had been waiting for me to find that letter. Not to punish me. Not even to hurt him. But to make sure the truth didn't die with her.

A few months passed before the next storm.

That's when my sister Julia's wedding started to loom on the calendar, and the cords began to tighten and knot in places I thought I'd already untangled.

In those months, I tried to live quietly. I threw myself into work, into errands, into the illusion of normalcy. I told myself that keeping busy was progress, that staying silent was peace. But silence isn't peace; it's pause. And I could feel the pause stretching thin.

He'd call, and I'd let it go to voicemail. I'd watch the screen light up with his name and wait for it to fade again. The sound of his voice, even in recordings, felt different now; too smooth, too measured, like someone reciting lines from a script he'd already perfected. Every "Hey" carried the echo of that letter I'd found, the one where he argued against my existence.

For the first time, I didn't feel guilt for ignoring him. I felt relief.

Distance was oxygen.

But distance never stays safe for long.

When the wedding invitations went out, reality came back sharp and clear. There was no avoiding it. We'd have to sit in the same room again, breathe the same air, share the same photographs, and pretend the same old performance still worked.

It would be my first time seeing him since finding the letter; the proof that I was never meant to exist, written in his own careful hand.

I wasn't ready to confront him. Not yet. The letter had given me power I didn't know what to do with. Truth sharp enough to cut him open, but heavy enough to wound me, too. I carried it quietly, folded in memory, like a weapon I didn't want to draw.

I told myself I'd be civil. I told myself it was for Julia. And for the most part, that was true.

But beneath the smile I rehearsed for her big day, there was something else building. Something colder, steadier.

Not revenge. Not even anger.

Recognition.

The next time I saw him, I would finally know exactly who I was sitting across from.

Chapter 10 – His God-Given Right

Some men build empires out of money or land. My father built his out of moments that were supposed to belong to other people.

He didn't need property deeds or titles; he just needed an audience. Weddings, birthdays, graduations, any place with a microphone or a captive crowd became bricks in the structure he'd been fortifying for decades.

My sister Julia had wanted something simple, yet elegant: an outdoor ceremony at the small, historic church she loved, followed by a lakeside reception under white tents with the people who truly supported her. It was meant to feel easy, intimate, safe. The kind of day you could exhale in.

She'd picked a soft color palette, handwrote her invitations, and kept saying she wanted "no drama, no surprises." She said it like a prayer.

She asked him to come. I still don't know if she truly wanted him there or just felt she had to invite him. Maybe she hoped that proximity could pass for peace, and that if you stood close enough to the storm, maybe it would mistake you for part of the calm.

In the weeks leading up to the wedding, he called her every day. Not quick check-ins. Like two-hour marathons that started as conversation and ended like interrogations. I could always tell when she'd just gotten off the phone with him. She would call me, her voice would shake, her sentences half-started, like she was still trying to calm her nervous system down.

Sometimes she'd try to laugh it off, "You know how he is," but her laugh never reached the end of the sentence.

After each call with him, she'd call me.

Her voice always came thin, brittle around the edges. She'd replay the latest incident like a confession: another argument that began with a question and ended with a verdict, another boundary he'd found a way to step over.

Sometimes it was small. His disapproval of her invite list, or his insistence that certain relatives deserved "special recognition." Other times it was bigger—his demand to approve the seating chart or to control who walked her down the aisle.

With him, even the smallest decisions became moral emergencies.

He had a gift for making joy feel like disobedience.

"He's freaking out about my choice of who I want walking me down the aisle. He wants to talk about the program and what he doesn't like about it."

"Just breathe," I told her. "This is your day. You are paying for everything. You have the final say."

The words sounded strong coming out of my mouth, but they felt powerless as soon as they hit the air. They were the same survival lines I'd used my whole life: minimize, soothe, de-escalate, hold space for the person he'd just torn through.

I sent her small jokes, gentle reminders that she was allowed to enjoy this, that she didn't have to keep managing him. But each message felt like bailing water from a boat with a hole in it.

I could see the exhaustion settling in her eyes every time I visited; the quiet kind that comes from trying to keep peace with someone who thrives on chaos.

She was radiant, though, in that way only brides can be when they're still trying to believe it will all work out. And I loved her for that hope. For still wanting a beautiful day in spite of him.

But I also knew what was coming.

You can't build anything on a fault line and expect it not to shift.

The day of the wedding smelled like spring flowers and cake, but the air itself felt tight, humming with the kind of nerves that come when certain people mistake an audience for love. Every surface gleamed, every ribbon tied perfectly. People smiled a little too wide, laughed a little too loud. Weddings are supposed to celebrate joining; this one felt like waiting for something to crack.

Everyone looked their best. My father looked like the man in a commercial about the perfect family with his hair neatly combed, jacket pressed, and smile rehearsed. His eyes were bright in that dangerous way they always were when he believed the spotlight belonged to him. When he stepped into the church, he didn't walk so much as survey; eyes sweeping the pews like a director inspecting his set before the cameras rolled. Even the ushers straightened their posture when he passed.

I felt the old reflex in my chest; the one that says make yourself small before he notices you. But this time, I didn't move. I sat in the second row, front and opposite, close enough to see him but far enough to breathe. I couldn't share a row with him, not after what I'd found. The word abortion still burned in my mind; blue ink seared behind my eyes like a watermark. Watching him play the part of the proud father felt obscene.

He scanned the crowd, waiting for his cue, the way he always did before a performance. The certainty in his posture made my stomach twist; he's going to do something, I thought. He always did.

One of their worst phone calls had ended in tears weeks earlier, after Julia told him she wanted her mom to walk her down the aisle. She'd tried to explain, gently, that she and Laura were close, that it simply felt right, and that her and dad have drifted apart over the years. But he couldn't hear that without twisting it into rejection. By the end, she was sobbing, and he was shouting that it was his God-given right for a father to walk his daughter down the aisle. The words had echoed through the phone loud enough that I'd heard them when she called me after, still crying, voice shaking as she said, "He just won't let it go."

So, when Julia finally appeared at the back of the church, arm linked with Laura's, both of them radiant and calm. It felt like defiance wrapped in grace. Every step she took down that aisle said this is my life, my choice. I remember the light filtering through the stained-glass windows, breaking across her dress in streaks of pink and gold. The air smelled like lilies and perfume. For the first time in a long while, I thought: maybe something ordinary and good can happen here.

Then I saw him move.

It wasn't subtle. He stood up with a suddenness that seemed rehearsed, the kind of timing only a man who loves drama can master. His brothers and sisters shifted in their seats, complicit bodyguards. A few even smiled, as if they'd known this was coming. I could almost hear the cue: and now, enter the father.

Gerald—Julia's stepfather and the officiant—was listed in the program beneath the bride's parents, along with Laura and my father. Alphabetical order had placed my father's name last. To most people, that would mean nothing. To him, it was blasphemy.

As the procession neared his row, he pushed past the cluster of relatives like a man reclaiming a prop. In one sweeping movement, he stepped into the narrow aisle and reached for her arm, wrapping it around his. Laura, mid-step, stumbled sideways, forced into the pews. There was a collective gasp—soft but sharp—the kind that ripples through a crowd before anyone understands what they've just witnessed.

The photographer's flash punctured the silence. Click. A small white burst caught his hand on her arm, her startled face, Laura's confusion. Each shutter was a tiny witness.

He had made room for himself by making her less stable.

The whole thing lasted maybe five seconds, but it felt eternal. Julia's eyes darted to her mother, then to the aisle ahead, and she kept walking because what else could she do? A bride shouldn't have to wrestle her father in her wedding dress.

He'd told everyone it was his "God-given right," and that tradition gave him authority—that "a father walks his daughter down the aisle." His siblings had agreed, nodding like a jury already convinced. Their version of family loyalty came wrapped in threats and sealed with silent approval.

They'd hated that Gerald's name had been printed at all. They said it was "disrespectful." It didn't matter that the names were alphabetical, that no one else cared. In his world, logic was irrelevant if his ego was wounded.

By the time the recessional began, the damage had already spread. You could feel it in the air—the tension buzzing just beneath the music. His relatives, tight-lipped and offended, whispered among themselves. A few stood, clutching purses and coats, and filed out of the church before the final hymn had even finished. They walked past guests who had come expecting cake and dancing, their expressions a mix of confusion and judgment. They didn't go to the reception. They didn't call to congratulate.

It was their way of sending a message: When he feels insulted, we all leave the event.

I watched them go, one after another, and felt something split cleanly inside me. Not surprise, not anger, just the confirmation of a truth I'd already known. He would ruin anything that didn't center him. And now, he'd done it again, this time dressed in a suit in church, under stained glass, before God and family.

Julia kept smiling through it, but her smile looked like a performance too—a bride pretending her father hadn't just turned her ceremony into a scene.

And somewhere in that silence, I realized I wasn't embarrassed for him anymore. I was embarrassed of him.

Later, the photos told the story better than anyone in the family ever would.

Every shot of Julia's face walking down the aisle was tainted by his interruption. Ruined. None of them could be used for the album.

What should have been a string of radiant moments turned into evidence; her face caught mid-shock, mouth tight with anger, the real smile gone for a heartbeat before the practiced one returned for the cameras. Laura's body twisted from the shove, and his hand clamped on Julia's arm like ownership. The camera, meant to capture her joy, became a silent witness to the second she stopped being the bride and became his prop.

When the proofs arrived a few weeks later, I sat with Julia and scrolled through them on her laptop. We both tried to laugh, but it came out thin and brittle. The photos flicked by in silence until we reached that sequence; her halfway down the aisle, his hand closing over hers, her smile breaking in two. "God," she whispered, half to herself, "you can see it happen."

And she was right. You could see it in her shoulders. The way they tensed, lifted, then dropped when she forced herself to keep walking. You could see it in the angle of Laura's body as she was pushed aside, trying to stay upright without ruining the moment. Even the light seemed different in those few frames, colder somehow, as if the air itself had stepped back.

People would tell themselves stories to make sense of it. He told the story of tradition. His brothers told the story of insult. His cousins told the story of pride. Guests whispered about confusion, calling it "unfortunate" or "awkward," their words smoothing over what really happened until it sounded like a misunderstanding instead of a choice.

But Julia and her circle remembered it for what it was: clumsy, selfish, and humiliating.

For me, watching her stumble under the weight of his need was a demonstration of what generosity had become in our family: not a debt that frees you, but a tether that keeps you moving where someone else wants you to. It was the same currency he'd used my whole life. Disguising control as love, obligation as care, and humiliation as tradition.

The reception carried on like a house after an argument: laughter too loud, music just a little offbeat, smiles that strained at the edges. Laura pretended nothing had happened, Julia clung to her new husband, and I spent the night wondering how a man could ruin something so pure and still believe he was right.

My sister's wedding was meant to be a day of kindness and new beginnings. Instead, it became an object lesson in how generosity can be hollowed out and used as a tether. He gave his blessing in the same breath he claimed prerogative; the gift and the claim arriving together, tied like a noose disguised as ribbon.

And in the end, it wasn't just the photos he ruined. He never did give my sister and brother-in-law their wedding gift.

He gave them a story instead—one that would outlast every plate, every centerpiece, every flower that wilted.

A story that would live in the photos, in the whispers, and in the ache that follows every family event where someone asks, "Remember when…"

Because that's what he always wanted.

Not to be remembered fondly; only to be remembered first.

Around that same time as the wedding, Dan reached out to me through Facebook Messenger, asking if I wanted to hang out sometime. His message was short and casual, but it landed like light in a dark room I hadn't realized I'd been sitting in. We'd met the year before through a mutual friend at a party, one of those nights where laughter felt effortless and I'd caught myself watching him longer than I meant to. He had an ease about him; something soft but grounded that made everything around him feel less jagged.

Even my mom had met him once. She'd liked him instantly.

After the wedding chaos, Dan's message felt like permission to start over. We started seeing each other more often. We dated for a few months before deciding to move in together. It wasn't rushed so much as practical. My mom's house had sold, and Dan's lease was ending, so we found a place that felt like a clean start for both of us. We decorated the place together, built IKEA furniture until midnight, and laughed over takeout on the floor surrounded by cardboard. It was the kind of domestic chaos that didn't end in shouting; just the sound of two people figuring out how to respectfully share space without breaking it.

Julia and Mike, my half-brother and half-sister, knew exactly who Dan was to me. I was out to them, and they were supportive in that unconditional way that meant everything. But Dad; I never told him. He never asked, and I never planned to tell him. I wasn't about to hand him the confirmation of what he'd already suspected all those years ago with the newspaper stunt. He didn't deserve that satisfaction. Some truths you keep sacred by refusing to let the wrong person touch them.

We only saw him about once a year for the obligatory Christmas dinner with my siblings. That was enough. Dan met him at one of those dinners and, after about an hour, leaned over to me and said quietly, "He's scary."

It stunned me how quickly he saw it.

How easily he read what I'd spent decades trying to name.

He noticed the same things I used to rationalize away: the clipped tone, the smirk that wasn't quite a smile, the way every question was really a trap.

For the first time, I felt truly validated. Someone outside the family saw the thing I had been screaming silently about for years and believed me without needing proof. That kind of recognition is its own kind of rescue.

Once Dan and I moved in together, that one dinner a year became the only time I saw my father or anyone from his side of the family. The calls slowed. The invitations also slowed.

Occasionally, an email or group message would come through about a birthday, graduation, or family get-together on his side; celebrations that sounded harmless on paper. Each time, I'd send polite excuses: work's been hectic, we already have plans, maybe next time. I couldn't bring myself to say the real reason out loud, that I wouldn't be there because my dad would be. It was easier to sound busy than to admit I was protecting my peace.

We didn't like being around him, and we didn't need to be. Our life together became small in the best way: grocery runs, weekend brunches, movie nights, the comfort of shared quiet. I was finally living my life on my own terms; finding some peace and enjoying the stillness of normal days with Dan. The silence in our home wasn't heavy anymore. It was safety. It was the sound of a life no longer lived on someone else's terms.

Then one night, he called.

The name and number lit up my phone like a flare from a place I'd been trying to escape. For a few seconds I almost didn't answer. But that's the thing about old training. You still pick up.

His voice was unusually soft, careful. The kind of tone he used when he needed something, when charm was his camouflage.

He said he was "in a bad spot" and needed a favor.

I could almost hear the capital F in it.

Growing up, I'd heard variations of that line for years. There was always a crisis just around the corner: a bill that hadn't been paid, a car that needed tires, a check that hadn't cleared. For a man who made his living arguing about responsibility, he never seemed to carry any himself.

He started with small talk—asked how work was going and if "I'd done anything fun lately." Then, as always, he shifted. "Listen," he said, sighing into the phone, "I wouldn't be asking if it weren't serious. I just need a little help. Things are tight right now. I need some money."

I waited for the number. It never came.

He said only, "A few thousand, at least."

He wanted me to take cash advances against my credit cards and promised it would be short-term. He'd make the payments. He'd cover the interest. He said all the right words in the right order, the same performance I'd heard since childhood. Even now, as an adult, it still worked. The guilt blooming first, then the reflex to fix.

I didn't like the idea. My credit cards were for emergencies, not rescues.

But his crises had always disguised themselves as emergencies. And deep down, part of me still wanted to be the son who could finally make him proud. So I told him I'd help.

After we hung up, I sat on the couch for a while, staring at the blank TV screen. The silence felt heavy with old patterns. I told Dan what had happened, half-defensive, half-ashamed, and he just nodded. "How much are you thinking?" he asked gently.

"Two thousand," I said. "That's all I'm comfortable with losing if he doesn't pay it back."

He didn't argue. He knew this wasn't really about money. It was about proving I could still do the right thing, even when right and wrong felt indistinguishable under his shadow.

Dan came with me that night. He didn't have to say why; he just said, "You shouldn't have to go alone."

That drive felt longer than it should have. The air was damp and cold, and the wipers squeaked across the glass like a pulse that wouldn't steady. I remember my hands gripping the steering wheel, the envelope of cash on the console between us, my name suddenly feeling too small for the moment.

My father had agreed to meet us at the bottom of his driveway. The same gravel incline that had haunted my childhood, the one where headlights hit nothing but trees and shadows, while the wild brush on each side sang scratches into the paint on the sides. The kind of darkness that swallows sound.

I pulled up and left my high beams on. The light cut up the hill, catching him mid-stride, frozen in the glare. For a second, he looked like a stranger; a man caught doing something he wasn't supposed to.

He couldn't even see Dan sitting in the passenger seat beside me; the beams made the interior a mirror. Maybe that was for the best. It made the scene feel like what it really was: a transaction between ghosts of who we used to be.

I got out, the gravel crunching under my shoes, and walked up the driveway about thirty feet to where he was standing.

The air smelled like cold earth and exhaust. I handed him the envelope.

He opened it immediately, thumbed through the bills, counting in silence. Then he looked up at me with that smirk I'd known since childhood, the one that meant he'd found the angle, the upper hand.

"Wow," he said, his voice edged with sarcasm. "I thought you were doing better at your job."

The words landed like a blade—quick, precise, familiar.

For a second, everything in me rebelled. I wanted to tell him to go to hell, to grab my money back right out of his hand, to remind him that no one else in his life would still answer that phone call.

But the words wouldn't come. They never did.

Instead, I swallowed hard and said, "That's what I could get quickly."

He grinned like I'd passed another test I didn't remember agreeing to take.

When I turned back toward the car, my legs felt heavy, the kind of heavy that comes from holding in too much. I kept my eyes straight ahead, watching my own shadow stretch long across the gravel.

I got in the car, shut the door, and sat in silence for a moment. The smell of the envelope still clung to my hands; paper and sweat.

Dan didn't say anything right away. He just stared through the windshield, watching my father's silhouette fade into darkness.

Finally, he said quietly, "He got what he wanted."

I nodded, feeling that old familiar ache, the one that always followed doing "the right thing" for a man who'd never deserved it.

A few months passed. Life settled back into its rhythms: work, dinners with Dan, laughter that felt like oxygen after years of holding my breath. For a while, it almost felt like that night at the end of his driveway had been just another bad dream. One more moment I could file away under things not worth reopening.

Then Christmas came.

We met at our usual restaurant, the same booth near the back where the lights were dim enough for pretending. It was our yearly ritual: one dinner a year, a polite performance of family unity that fooled no one. I arrived with Dan, who'd learned to play his part with quiet dignity; handshakes, small talk, and strategic smiles. My father was already there, coat draped over the chair beside him, his posture confident as ever.

We ordered. We talked about safe topics: the weather, traffic, whatever game was playing on the bar's television. He was unusually calm, as though the previous months hadn't existed. Then, halfway through the meal, he reached into his jacket pocket and pulled out an envelope.

He slid it across the table like a lawyer passing evidence.

"Here you go," he said casually.

Inside was a check, repayment for the $2,000 loan, plus interest.

For a moment I couldn't speak. He'd actually kept his word.

It shouldn't have felt like a miracle, but it did.

I thanked him out of habit, not gratitude, and tucked the envelope away. Dan reached under the table and touched my knee once, a silent anchor.

Even so, it wasn't the money that stayed with me. It was the memory of that night under the high beams. The way he'd turned a plea for help into a stage for condescension. The way he'd managed to take kindness and make it feel like weakness. He had a gift for flipping every gesture upside down until you doubted your own goodness. That was his real debt, the one he'd never repay.

We kept that holiday routine for a few more years. One dinner a year. Just enough to keep the peace. Each meal had its script: surface-level conversation, a few cautious laughs, an early exit before the tension found its footing. I always drove home afterward feeling the same numb exhaustion, like I'd been speaking a language that didn't belong to me.

And yet, outside those dinners, my life was changing. Slowly, beautifully, defiantly.

Dan and I built our own world: movie nights, road trips, and the comfort of shared silence. We learned each other's rhythms in the kind of quiet that didn't demand anything. He'd make coffee before I woke up; I'd leave notes by his keys before work. It was ordinary in the best way. After years of chaos, I started to understand that peace could be loud too—it just hummed differently.

Then the world shifted.

It was June 26, 2015. The Supreme Court ruled that marriage equality was the law of the land.

For the first time, love like mine wasn't something whispered; it was recognized, protected, and written into history. I remember standing in the living room with Dan, both of us staring at the news on TV, too stunned to move. He turned to me, smiling through tears, and said, "We're real now."

I hadn't realized until that moment how much I'd been holding my breath for something I'd never expected to happen. For once, the law wasn't his—it was ours.

That summer, we decided it was our turn.

We got engaged!

And I knew one of the next few times my father saw me, it would be at my wedding.

That thought alone was enough to make my pulse quicken. The memory of Julia's wedding still burned behind my eyes: him stepping into the aisle, grabbing her arm, stealing her moment under the guise of tradition. I could still see the flash of cameras catching her shock, the forced smile she wore to survive it. If he could turn her day into theater, what might he do with mine?

I didn't want him there. Every instinct in me said don't invite him. But family pressure has a way of whispering in your ear that it'll be fine, he wouldn't dare this time, you might regret it if you don't try.

The problem was, I knew him.

Daring was what he did best.

And yet, love was finally something I could claim in the open. For the first time, I had something pure, something untouched by his reach. And I wasn't about to let his shadow crawl down that aisle or turn my vows into another performance.

This time, if he tried to make a scene, the cameras wouldn't capture my silence.

They'd capture the moment he learned the show was over and I would tell him to leave, in front of everyone.

And just in case, my best man was ready. He knew the story, knew the patterns, knew what I'd been through. Before the ceremony, he put a hand on my shoulder and said quietly, "If your dad even breathes wrong during your vows, I'll take care of it—and I don't mind spending the night in jail for you."

It was amazing and somewhat relieving to realize that I wasn't the only one standing guard anymore.

Chapter 11 – A Wedding and a War

We'd spent months planning every small detail and had fun along the whole way, trying to make the day foolproof. But there are some things you can't plan for, especially when the person who taught you chaos gets a front-row seat.

We had no idea that all the peace we'd built into that day would be tested before the first dance even began.

Dan and I sat at the kitchen table surrounded by envelopes, cardstock, and a mess of metallic pens that kept rolling off the edge. Even the laser printer had been relocated to the kitchen island so we could print waterproof labels in handwriting font, just in case the envelopes got wet. We were building a wedding from scratch; two men who finally could. The Supreme Court's decision had come the year before, and it still felt new, fragile, like a miracle you didn't want to touch too hard.

Every small choice felt like defiance in the best way possible. Picking fonts, comparing shades of crimson ribbon, deciding between "Mr. and Mr." or simply our names; it was both ordinary and revolutionary. The world hadn't caught up yet, but in our kitchen that night, it already had.

We'd already chosen the venue—a restored barn with wide-plank floors and beams that caught the late-afternoon sun just right. The ceremony would take place outside, framed by fall trees that looked like they'd been painted on, with shades of yellow, orange, and red. Inside, there wasn't quite enough space for everyone, so we planned overflow tables upstairs, tucked near the railings where guests could look down at the dance floor. It was perfect, and it was ours for that one special day.

I remember Dan sketching a rough seating chart on the back of a takeout menu, his handwriting looping around coffee rings. We talked about who would sit where, who needed to be kept apart, and who might surprise us by getting along. Every name felt like a small knot we were either tying or untying. Planning a wedding is really just planning how love will exist in public.

Every night for a week, we sorted through the guest list, debating who to include, who to let go. It felt like the adult version of building a life; every decision carrying weight, and every name attached to a history. When we finally hit the venue's capacity, we leaned back in our chairs, exhausted but proud.

Dan handled the RSVP cards and envelopes. I worked on stuffing the envelopes and applying the labels. We mailed them out in batches, after we'd double-checked everyone's addresses. We even called people ahead of time to make sure they'd know before the mail carrier did; just a small courtesy that made it feel even more real. Everyone was thrilled. Friends cheered. Family sent messages of love. For the first time in a long time, the future didn't feel like something I had to survive. It felt like something I was allowed to look forward to.

The night we dropped the final stack of envelopes into the blue mailbox on the corner, we stood there a moment longer than necessary. It felt ceremonial, like sending pieces of ourselves into the world with return addresses. We held hands, laughed about how domestic we'd become, and then drove back home under the stars, talking about playlists and centerpieces and whether or not the DJ would understand what "no Nickelback songs" really meant.

Planning became its own kind of language between us. We spoke in tasks and timelines, but what we were really saying was I'm in this with you. And for me, after years of walking on eggshells and waiting for explosions, that steady kind of love felt like a luxury I hadn't known how to dream about.

I didn't realize then how much that peace would mean. How much it would need defending once the RSVPs started coming in.

Because even perfect plans can't keep old storms from finding their way back.

Everyone, it seemed, was excited; except one person.

I hadn't called my father before mailing the invitation. He didn't deserve the satisfaction of hearing it from me. The confirmation of what he'd suspected since that old newspaper stunt. He could read the invitation for himself. I wanted the envelope to do the talking this time, the embossed script on the front spelling out a truth he'd always tried to rewrite: I was marrying a man, and I didn't need his permission.

Weeks passed, and the RSVPs started arriving in the mailbox one by one. Each card felt like a small heartbeat of joy, proof that our love was being witnessed. We'd spread them out on the table, arranging the little ivory rectangles into neat rows; friends, coworkers, distant relatives. We marked everyone's response on their row in our Excel spreadsheet. Some wrote little notes on the back: Can't wait! or Finally! or Bring tissues. We laughed at the ones who picked "chicken" even though we knew they were vegetarians, and smiled at the ones who chose "fish" because they thought it sounded fancy.

Every envelope that came in felt like an exhale after years of holding my breath. We'd made it this far. We were building something real.

All except one.

His.

I told myself I didn't care, that it didn't matter whether he came or not. But every morning when I opened the mailbox, part of me still looked for his handwriting; the neat loopy print that had once signed every letter he penned to my mom. It never came.

Days passed. Then a week. Finally, I sighed and said to Dan, "Damn, I have to call him."

I dialed. He answered on the second ring.

"Hey," I said lightly, though my pulse was thudding in my ears. "Just checking, did you get a wedding invitation in the mail?"

"Yes," he said.

And then silence.

The kind that stretches out, heavy and deliberate, waiting for you to fill it. It was a silence I knew too well—the pause that said I'm still the one in control here.

I pressed on. "Okay, just wanted to make sure it arrived. I didn't see the RSVP yet."

More silence.

He was doing it again. Weaponizing quiet the way other people used words. He didn't need to raise his voice to remind me who had written the script of our old conversations: he just had to wait.

Then, finally: "Is my family invited?"

The question landed like a test. Not curiosity. Accusation.

I told him no, gently but clearly. I explained that the venue was small, that I hadn't seen most of the aunts, uncles, or cousins in years, and there just wasn't room. Adding his side of the family would be around thirty more people, and the space and budget couldn't stretch that far.

His tone shifted, sharp and wounded. "How could you do this? They would want to be there for you."

There it was. The familiar inversion. He wasn't angry because they'd been excluded. He was angry because he hadn't been the one to include them.

I could feel the old heat rising in my chest, that familiar pull to defend, to explain, to fix. My instincts screamed to make it right, to calm the situation, to shrink myself into something easier to love. Instead, I said, "I have to go," and hung up.

I sat there for a long time afterward, staring at the phone in my hand, the silence in the room pressing in on me like static. Dan reached across the table and squeezed my hand once; no words, just that grounding touch that said you don't owe him peace.

The next night, the phone rang again. His name lit up the screen. I thought about ignoring it, but old habits die hard. I answered.

He said one of my cousins, someone I'd been close with growing up, was really upset about not being invited and was thinking about showing up at my wedding anyway. I could almost hear the satisfaction in his voice, the way he'd positioned himself as the messenger of someone else's disappointment.

I told Dad to tell him sorry, and that he couldn't just show up. There wasn't room, the venue would charge us extra, and I couldn't add people at the last minute for meals.

He said, "Well, I can't tell him no."

Something in me snapped. Years of swallowing words, of folding myself small enough to fit his expectations, rose up all at once.

"Then I guess I'll have to hire security," I said, my voice low and flat.

He didn't like that answer, so we hung up again.

A few nights later, he called again. Same dance. The pattern had become predictable: his long silences, my attempts to fill them, and his questions laid out like traps. Each time, I found myself speaking louder, defending my choices with more conviction—until he flipped the script. Suddenly I was "yelling," I was "defensive." He'd say things like, "You're never like this." "This isn't you at all." "I thought you were happy to get married."

I calmed myself down quickly to play his game again. Then, I reminded him that I still hadn't received his RSVP or a meal choice. Silence again. That studied, punishing quiet. The kind that wasn't really silence at all; it was performance. He'd perfected it long ago. Every pause was a reminder of how easily he could make me doubt myself.

At that point, I told Dan I was heading to the garage because I might start yelling. I didn't want to carry that energy into the new house we'd built together. Our home was supposed to be clean air and open space, not filled with ghosts of old conversations that always ended the same way, with me apologizing for things I didn't do.

I stepped into the garage, the cool air hitting me like a reset. The faint smell of paint and wood still lingered from when we'd finished unpacking. I shut the door behind me and leaned against the workbench, the phone pressed to my ear.

I could hear his voice through the receiver, smooth and casual, like he was just making small talk before he landed the punch.

"So," he said, dragging it out, "who's the girl in your relationship?"

It took a moment for my brain to catch up. The words hung there, absurd and cutting at the same time. "What? That doesn't even make sense—we're both men," I said, my voice rising louder and louder with each syllable.

He got loud too. Accusing me of being defensive again. Telling me I was "never like this before." His tone carried that familiar mixture of superiority and mock innocence, as if I were the one rewriting history.

The gaslighting was instant, automatic. It was muscle memory for him. He'd done it for so long that he didn't even have to think about it. The words came out smooth, practiced, rehearsed from years of being the man who always had to win.

I told him I had to go and hung up. My hands were shaking, not from fear, but from fury. A clean, sharp anger that didn't spiral, it focused. It wasn't about him anymore. It was about me finally refusing to play the game.

I stood there for a moment, breathing hard, the hum of the garage freezer filling the space. Then I walked back inside, where the light was warm and steady, and the man I loved sat quietly on the couch, his eyes soft with understanding.

I sat down beside him, picked up my father's RSVP card, and checked the box marked Vegan. He'd never in his life choose that option, and he'd hate every bite of it. Then, with a slow, deliberate smile, I placed him at a table with guests whose political views couldn't have been further from his, and who were never shy about sharing them.

It was a small act of rebellion, but it made me ridiculously happy.

Dan laughed when he saw it. "That's evil, and I love it" he said, half-joking.

"Maybe," I said. "But it's also allowing me to smile after that call."

The morning of our wedding arrived crisp and gold, the kind of fall day that felt almost staged, with sunlight threading through autumn leaves, the air clean and sharp like new paper. The sky was so clear it felt rehearsed, as if the universe had taken direction just for us.

We got to the venue early, a little jittery but giddy in that way only people in love can be. Everything smelled faintly of wood smoke and pine, the barn still holding traces of last night's chill. The gravel crunched beneath our shoes as we unloaded the last boxes from the car: place cards, programs, extra candles, favors for each guest; all the finishing touches that make a dream tangible.

Inside the barn, strings of Edison lights hung like constellations, glowing softly against the raw wood beams. The tables gleamed with their simple centerpieces; glass jars, wildflowers, and tiny tea lights flickering like fireflies. The space felt alive but calm, touched by the kind of peace you can't buy or fake. It smelled like cinnamon and autumn air, like something homemade and right.

The photographer moved around us quietly, clicking through each detail: ties straightened, boutonnieres pinned, the soft chaos of people laughing and half-dressed in the background. The photos from those first hours turned out beautifully. They were full of motion and nerves and that particular morning light that makes everything look like hope.

And then I saw him.

My father had arrived. I saw him through the window.

For a moment, I actually smiled. Not out of warmth, but because I was almost excited for the show that awaited him: his vegan meal and the subtle political discomfort I'd scripted for him. It was petty, sure, but it felt like justice in miniature form, with the universe briefly letting me hold the pen.

He stood off to the side, close enough to be seen but not close enough to belong. His posture was too casual, too performative, the way someone stands when they know eyes are on them. The photographer caught sight of him and, without understanding the gravity of the moment, beckoned him closer for a few family shots.

"Let's get one with your dad," she said brightly, as if it were an ordinary request.

He walked over, smiling that too-wide smile of his, the kind that showed every tooth but none of the truth. I could feel my pulse thudding in my ears as the photographer positioned us. The barn suddenly felt smaller. My skin prickled beneath the collar of my shirt.

"Shake hands," she instructed, "and look at each other for a moment while I snap a few pictures."

I hesitated. Every muscle in me wanted to resist. My stomach tightened. It felt like being a kid again—cornered, on display, waiting for him to find something to criticize. Even standing there in my wedding suit, surrounded by laughter and love, my body still remembered the command: Don't make him angry.

When our hands met, his grip was too firm, performative, like a stage direction he wanted everyone to notice. I looked into his eyes, and it felt like looking through glass; cold, reflective, giving nothing back. And in that instant, I wasn't a groom anymore. I was a son standing in front of a man who had made fear feel like air.

For a heartbeat, I actually braced for it. Waiting for him to say something cruel, or whisper something just loud enough for me to hear. My smile faltered.

The photographer lowered her camera slightly, her expression shifting. She must've seen it: the stiffness, the way my shoulders had tensed, the flicker of panic that didn't belong in a wedding photo. Her voice softened.

"Okay," she said quietly, "we're good for now."

I stepped back, exhaling so hard it almost sounded like relief. He lingered there a second longer, pretending not to notice the way I turned away.

Relief flooded me as the photographer turned her lens toward someone else. For a few minutes, the day felt mine again, the leaves still glowing outside, the laughter still carrying from the barn, and the promise of everything that was about to begin.

I didn't realize until later how visible it must have been; that tiny fracture in the moment, the shadow slipping across my face just as the shutter clicked. You can't always spot trauma in a photograph, but sometimes, if you look closely, it's there. Caught in the hesitation between breaths, in the way a smile falters for half a second. We bought the CD of all the wedding photos afterward, but those shots weren't there. Either they were deleted for being unusable, or the photographer recognized the truth in my expression and quietly decided it wasn't meant to be preserved.

Guests began to arrive and take their seats, the chatter softening into a low, melodic hum as the music started. I watched from a distance, heart thudding in rhythm with the piano. The tension I'd been holding all morning finally loosened slightly. It was time.

Dan walked down the aisle with his mom, proud and steady, his steps sure in a way that made my chest ache. The autumn light caught the edge of his suit jacket, turning it gold for an instant. I'd seen him a thousand times before, but in that moment, it felt like seeing him for the first time—the person I'd been building toward my whole life.

I followed a few minutes later with Carol, my mom's best friend. She was the woman who'd known me my whole life and loved me without conditions. She had that calm, maternal energy that steadied me when I needed it most. As we stepped into the aisle, she squeezed my arm gently, whispering, "She'd be so proud of you."

Having her by my side felt right, like carrying a small piece of my mom with me. And I know for a fact that my mother would have wanted her to walk me down the aisle in her absence. The guests rose, the leaves overhead whispered in the soft wind, and for a moment I felt her there; my mother; woven into the air itself, watching me walk toward something she'd always hoped I'd find.

Gerald, Laura's husband, officiated the ceremony. He did an incredible job. Warm, calm, and full of humor and love that set everyone at ease. His voice carried through the crisp afternoon air, wrapping around the laughter and quiet sniffles of the guests. The ceremony itself was beautiful. When he pronounced us "husbands for life," the crowd erupted in cheers.

We kissed, our hands trembling slightly from adrenaline, and then walked back down the aisle together behind everyone. It felt unreal, like the kind of peace you only imagine as a kid but never quite believe will belong to you.

I'd worried, of course, that my dad might say something when the officiant asked if anyone objected. That pause, only half a second, maybe less, felt like an eternity. My best man turned around to watch my dad. I was waiting for him to run towards my father. Thankfully, it never came to that.

During the cocktail hour, the photographer pulled us aside for nearly forty-five minutes of photos. We slipped away to a patch of golden light behind the barn while guests mingled outside with drinks and hors d'oeuvres. From where we stood, I could hear the murmur of laughter, the clinking of glasses, and the faint strum of acoustic guitar drifting through the cool breeze. Everything about the afternoon felt impossibly soft and golden, like the world had been temporarily rewritten in our favor.

When we finally came back inside, the evening was already unfolding beautifully. The candles had been lit, and the barn glowed with warmth; the kind of light that makes even strangers look like family.

We made our entrances to the songs we'd chosen, each one tailored to the personality of our friends. Some were hilarious, a few sentimental, and all of them perfectly us. When it came time for our turn, the room filled with applause and the rhythmic clinking of glasses. I could feel the vibration of joy in the air, this collective exhale of love and support.

We took our seats at the head table, smiling as speeches began. They were kind, funny, and emotional, with words that left us both teary-eyed. Dan's dad talked about love and how he now has another son. My sister told the story of how I'd met Dan and ended it with how proud my mom would have been to be in attendance. The sniffles and laughter that followed was the kind that dissolves tension completely, replacing it with something tender.

Dinner arrived soon after. Between bites and conversations, I caught movement at one of the tables; table number four. A quiet disruption. My dad.

He was sending back his plate and arguing with the server. Even from across the room, I could see the way he gestured with his hand—firm, entitled, the same tone he used when ordering people around in court or his house. The vegan plate. He was trying to swap it for beef or chicken, anything except the vegan meal.

I kept my expression neutral, smiling politely through a conversation at our table, but inside, I felt something rare: victory. A small one, but it counted. It wasn't about revenge. It was about balance. About seeing, for once, the consequence meet the behavior.

Dan glanced at me, following my gaze. When he saw it too, he gave a knowing smile. "Guess he doesn't like lentils," he whispered.

"Guess not," I said, taking another sip of margherita.

After dinner, we started making our way from table to table, shaking hands, hugging guests, and thanking everyone for coming. Every face we passed was glowing with joy, laughter, or a little too much champagne. The air smelled of wine and vanilla cake, of wood smoke and warmth.

And then we reached table number four. His table.

Dan went first, extending his hand like he always did: open, composed, the kind of calm that made other people settle. My father took it, smiling tightly; the smile that showed the teeth and not the warmth. They exchanged the usual polite lines. I watched Dan's posture the whole time, the way he leaned in just enough to be kind but not so far as to invite trouble.

Then it was my turn.

I walked up with the practiced grin of someone who'd rehearsed this particular choreography in his head for years. I did the same; forced the calmness I didn't feel, pressed my palm into his, and tried to lengthen the moment into something ordinary. We swapped small talk about how great the food was, how lovely everything looked, neutral things that could be said without opening any old scabs. He nodded, answered, and then, because we were at a wedding where civility is currency, he asked about the open bar, so I told him to enjoy it, and that we paid for the bar to be opened all night. It felt ridiculous and deliberate: a politeness offered like a test that I was determined not to fail.

We moved on, shaking more hands, greeting more people. I felt the skin of my palms warm and then cool as if my body were recalibrating to normal. Around me, laughter kept folding the day into itself: plates clinking, someone telling an inside joke, a child squealing. The barn hummed with the tidy happiness of other people's joy, and I clung to it like a raft.

Our first dance followed; a pop song that had always felt like ours. When the first notes started, the room narrowed to a soft circle around us. Spotlights skimmed over the edges of the floor, making everything outside of that circle fall away. Dan's hand rested at the small of my back; my hand fit in the crook of his shoulder like it had been carved for that exact shape. For those minutes, the future we'd been sketching in our kitchen became a thing you could stand inside. The world spun softly at the margin, and for a while, I believed, utterly, that the day could remain unbroken.

Afterward came cake—perfect, sweet, and gone too fast. Then more dancing, the playlists we'd agonized over spinning us into silly, sweaty joy. People hugged us; someone tossed a napkin into the air like confetti. The barn flickered with movement and sound, and I tasted sugar, champagne, and the soft echo of everything we had planned to be perfect. To cap it off, we opened the Mac and Cheese bar, piled high with toppings to help everyone soak up what they'd been drinking.

A few times that night, I noticed both of my sisters off to the side, crying together. They weren't loud; more like two people trying to share a hurt so it won't explode. I tried to ask what happened, but they wouldn't tell me. "Nope," Julia said, wiping her eyes and forcing a smile that didn't reach them. "This is your night. You're going to enjoy it."

I wanted to press. I wanted to know what had wrung them so suddenly. But there are some things you can't interrupt with questions without breaking the spell for everyone else, and weddings feel like fragile ecosystems where a single loud thing can unbalance everything. So I folded the worry into my pocket and smiled for the cameras, let the music pull me back into the safe choreography of the evening.

Later, as things wound down, I saw them getting ready to leave after saying their goodbyes; Julia heading to her car and Theresa pulling in to pick up Anna. Dan and I ran outside to walk them to their cars, thanking them again for coming, and calling out promises to catch up the next day. The parking lot smelled like cold asphalt and spilled drink, the night air pin-prick sharp.

Anna's mom arrived first, and they hugged goodbye. I asked Julia to tell us what happened again, gently this time, thinking a private word in the parking lot might make it easier. Then Julia turned toward me, her face tight, furious and small all at once.

"I can't tell you right now," she said through gritted teeth. "But if Dad walks out here in this parking lot, I'm going to run him over."

Her voice was low and dangerous in a way I'd never heard from her. The anger was real, radiating outward like heat so immediate I felt it under my own skin. It wasn't a joke. I begged her to tell us what had happened, any tiny clue, and she shook her head hard.

"Not on your wedding night," she said. "I'll call you tomorrow."

She didn't have to say more. The way she held herself, the way she watched the barn doors as if expecting him to appear, the tremor in her jaw; those things told me everything: whatever had happened inside had been sharp enough to bruise her.

Dad never came outside. He stayed where he had been. Inside, where he could stage and posture and be seen without leaving himself vulnerable. The night ended beautifully for us. The remaining guests left with warm, tired smiles and promises to send photos, to meet for brunch, to talk about the next time we'd all be together.

After the guests had gone, we got in the shuttle and headed back to the hotel for the after-party our friends had planned. There was more laughter, more champagne, a bass line that made the floor vibrate a little, and finally, blessedly, sleep. We collapsed into the hotel bed exhausted in the best possible way, hands still entangled, the day finally surrendering its last adrenaline to our breathing. The world outside the window was quiet, and for a few hours, the house of sleep held us like a shield.

The next morning, we packed our suits, cards, and gifts into the car and drove home, still riding the high of everything that had gone right. The air felt lighter than it had in months, with our windows down and coffee cups in the cupholders. We were heading home as a legally married couple. The world looked different in that afterglow, like it was tilting in our favor at last.

Then Julia called.

Her name lit up on the screen, and before I even answered, a small part of me braced.

She asked how the rest of the night had gone, and I told her it was perfect, because it had been. The ceremony, the laughter, the dancing, the after party, the way everything had stayed intact despite all the possibilities for chaos. I could still feel the rhythm of it in my body, like music that hadn't faded yet.

She hesitated before speaking again. I could hear her breathing through the line.

"Your wedding was so beautiful," she said finally, her voice gentle but edged. "But… there were a few things I learned about Dad yesterday."

The joy in my chest stilled.

She apologized for how angry she'd been when we'd last talked, said she'd tried to calm down before calling, but that she was still fuming. Then she told me why.

She'd heard that Dad had been telling other guests that Laura had paid for the wedding, and that this was supposedly the reason none of his family had been invited.

The lie hit me like static, irritating but not surprising. He'd always hated Laura after the divorce. She was one of the few people who saw through him early, who refused to play his games. Even now, he couldn't stop trying to turn people against her. The pattern was so familiar it almost felt scripted: diminish, distort, divide.

Looking back, I realized that's probably why he'd fabricated the disgusting "pedophile" rumor years ago—to drive a wedge between Laura and me. Even now, after all the damage, he was still chasing new fractures to make.

But that wasn't even the worst of it.

Julia's tone changed. I could hear the quiver under it—the kind that comes from trying to hold rage and heartbreak in the same breath.

She said that Anna had gone up to Laura and Gerald during the reception to say hello. She'd almost backed out, apparently, nerves getting the better of her. Julia told me that right before she walked over, Anna had whispered, "It's okay—they don't have to say hi if they don't want to."

Julia asked her why they wouldn't want to.

Anna said that Dad had told her, years ago, that Laura and Gerald hated her. That they always had.

The words made my stomach drop.

She grew up believing that—that two people who had barely known her despised her for existing. Imagine being a kid and carrying that around like luggage, believing you'd been rejected before you even had a chance to be known.

Julia said that when Anna finally approached them, she realized almost instantly it wasn't true. Laura's face had lit up the moment she saw her. She and Gerald had hugged her, talked with her, told her how proud they were of the woman she was becoming. They'd only ever wished her well. They offered advice about her future, smiling the whole time.

When Anna walked away from that conversation, she broke down crying. Julia said it wasn't the kind of crying you comfort. It was the kind that comes from years of believing a lie that's finally been dragged into daylight.

That lie—one so cruel and pointless—had kept Anna from knowing people who would've loved her. It was another wedge. Another manipulation. The kind of psychological vandalism he was best at.

Julia paused, her voice tightening again. Then she said that Anna had confessed something else that night; something she'd never told anyone before.

When they were kids, Dad used to make Anna run laps around his house when it was only her and him at the house. He told her that if she wanted to be popular like Julia, she needed to lose weight, and that running laps would be "good for her."

I went completely still. The steering wheel felt foreign in my hands.

It made Julia furious, she said. Furious that she hadn't known. Furious that it had been happening in the same house she grew up in, just out of sight. Furious that Anna, who had always been gentle, had carried that shame alone.

She told me she'd never seen Anna cry that hard.

The line went quiet for a while. Neither of us spoke. There was nothing left to say that could shrink what he'd done.

I looked out at the road ahead—the same Pennsylvania sun that had felt so warm a few minutes ago now glaring, flat, unkind.

In that silence, it hit me again that people like him never really stop. They just find new ways to rearrange the damage.

And somehow, even after all these years, we were still finding the pieces.

Later that day, my Nana called.

Her voice carried that familiar brightness, the same tone she used whenever she wanted to lift everyone else up. She told me how much she'd loved the wedding, said it was her favorite one she'd ever attended, and that the food was the best she'd ever had. She laughed as she said it, the sound soft and musical through the speaker. For a few moments, everything felt light again. I could picture her sitting at her kitchen table, the corded wall phone in one hand, a glass of iced tea in the other, her nails still polished from the day before.

Her husband hadn't come. After speaking with his Baptist pastor, he'd decided he shouldn't attend a wedding between two men.

Nana came anyway. She'd dressed beautifully, in a navy-blue dress with a pearl pin she'd said once was "for good luck." She'd glowed with pride the entire evening, sitting through every song, every speech, every toast with the kind of steady joy that makes people around her soften. When we exchanged vows, I saw her dab at her eyes with a folded napkin, smiling as if she could will her happiness across the distance between us.

It meant more to me than I could ever tell her; that she showed up, that she chose love over doctrine. That she refused to let someone else's rulebook decide who deserved to be celebrated. Her presence had been a quiet rebellion all its own, a sermon without words.

For a while, her call carried that same warmth. We laughed about how many people had danced like they'd been training for it all year. It was the kind of easy, post-wedding conversation you want to live in forever; the debrief of joy, the replay of moments that already feel like memories.

But as light as that call began, it didn't stay that way for long.

Before we hung up, Nana's voice shifted slightly, still gentle, but slower, like she was trying to decide whether to say what came next.

"Jeff, I probably shouldn't even mention this, but it is something that you should probably know" she began softly, "your father spoke to me during the reception."

My stomach sank before she even finished the sentence.

She went on to explain that he'd approached her at her table, one of his quiet ambushes; the kind that always came disguised as conversation. The kind where his voice stayed low and polite so no one around would suspect anything was wrong.

He'd told her that Dan's parents must have paid for the wedding since none of his family had been invited.

Even surrounded by joy, he couldn't resist spreading rot.

I could picture it perfectly: the faux-concerned tilt of his head, the calculated tone, the way he would lace a lie with just enough truth to make it plausible. The kind of poison that doesn't burn right away, it seeps.

Nana, bless her, said she'd just smiled and changed the subject. But the damage wasn't in what she believed. It was in knowing he'd tried. That even on the one day meant to be untouched by him, he'd found a crack to slip through.

The call ended kindly, her voice full of love again, but when I set the phone down, the quiet that followed felt heavier than it had all morning.

Over the next few days, friends began calling with the same story. Their voices were cheerful at first, full of congratulations, telling us how much fun they'd had, how beautiful the barn looked, how tender the vows had been, and how it had felt like the whole night had glowed from the inside out.

But then, always, came the same shift in tone.

They'd pause, lower their voice, and say, "Something was off about your dad."

When I asked what they meant, the answers blurred together in variations of the same scene: he'd been moving from table to table, introducing himself to people, telling them he was my father, as if anyone had asked. Between pleasantries, he'd slip in small complaints, little rewrites of reality. He told them that Dan hadn't even had the decency to shake his hand that night.

He was rewriting the story again, one conversation at a time, the way he always had; turning moments of his own discomfort into tales of someone else's wrongdoing. It wasn't enough for him to attend; he needed to narrate.

Anna, who had been seated next to him, confirmed it all. Every word. She recounted his tone, his posture, the forced lightness that carried something sour underneath. Then she stopped herself mid-sentence, her tone changing like a door closing.

"There's something else," she said quietly. "Something he said to me. I can't repeat it."

I pressed her, over and over, pleading with her to please tell me, but she wouldn't. Even now, a decade later when I ask her about what he said, she still won't.

All she'd say was, "The gist of it was… it would've been easier if you'd married a girl."

That sentence hung in the air long after the call ended. It felt like an echo from another lifetime, the same cruelty, just dressed in wedding clothes. For years afterward, I replayed that day, wondering if he'd managed to leave a mark on it, like some invisible stain that only I could see.

But time has a way of sharpening perspective. It pares things down to their truth. He didn't ruin anything. He only proved, one last time, that chaos was the only language he ever learned.

The wedding was never his story to tell. The light through the trees, the laughter that carried long into the night, the people who showed up and stayed—that's what remains. When I look back at the photos now, I don't see him. I see the joy he couldn't touch. I see the family I built from love, not obligation.

For once, he was just a guest. A guest who couldn't even stomach the vegan dinner I'd assigned him, and who talked the caterer into bringing out a meat dish instead. It figured. Even at my wedding, he couldn't follow the plan. But for a brief moment, I'd interrupted his script, and that was enough.

He also taught me storms, but I learned stillness.

He built walls, and I built a life.

And even now, a decade later, when I think of that day, I don't remember his rumors or his absence of grace.

I remember the air turning gold, the way the sunlight caught Dan's smile, the sound of our vows echoing through the open field. I remember the way the guests laughed when the DJ missed his cue, the taste of champagne and autumn air, the way the world felt unbreakable for once.

And above all, I remember the moment I finally understood.

I had walked through his shadow and still found the sun.

Chapter 12 – The Afterparty and the Unset Chairs

December 2016.

A month after our wedding.

The air had that early-winter stillness, the kind that makes everything feel both settled and waiting. Mornings were quiet, the kind of quiet that comes after joy, when the noise fades and all that's left is the soft hum of normal life returning.

I'd just begun to come down from the high of the ceremony; the music, the warmth, the faces that had filled the barn with light. The glow of it lingered like an afterimage. Sometimes I'd scroll through the photos late at night, still half-convinced the joy might fade if I didn't look at it often enough. For the first time in years, my life felt steady. The air around me didn't vibrate with tension. Even the silence felt safe.

Around that time, Julia told me she'd decided to cut Dad off completely, and I fully supported her decision.

She said it was the best thing she could do for herself and her family. Their conversations had stopped being pleasant a long time ago. They were just arguments now, circular and exhausting. Every talk with him felt like being pulled into a maze with no exit, where reason had no map.

Julia had always been strong-willed, but something in her had shifted. She wasn't giving him the reactions he wanted anymore. She wasn't engaging. She wasn't explaining or apologizing or trying to make him see her side.

She wouldn't be controlled, and he knew it.

His tactics had stopped working on her.

It was strange, and a little awe-inspiring, to watch someone else win the battle I'd spent years just trying to survive. She wasn't just setting boundaries; she was holding them. And somehow, watching her do it made me realize how much of my own energy had been spent managing his moods, walking the invisible tightrope between defiance and guilt.

Then my father called me.

The timing felt deliberate, like he could sense when calm had finally settled and couldn't stand not being at the center of my attention.

He said he wanted to have a get-together for his family. A kind of make-up celebration, since they hadn't been invited to the wedding. His tone was casual, almost generous, as if he were offering me a favor.

"It'll be at your place," he said, like it had already been decided.

He'd cook at his house, bring food, and make it a small thing, with just his family, nothing formal. The word family hung in the air like bait.

I didn't want it. Every part of me tensed at the idea of opening my door to people who had spent years pretending not to see me. But somehow, I found myself agreeing. I always did, back then. That was the magic trick. He made things sound like obligations disguised as opportunities.

I told myself it would be harmless, that it might even be good for him to see the first house that Dan and I had built, to see that my life didn't need his approval. But under that rationalizing voice, something smaller and older whispered, you should have said no.

A few days later, he called again.

"Your aunt wants to talk to you," he said. "She just wants you to know she's okay with the person you married."

The line went dead before I could respond. A few minutes later, the phone rang again.

Her voice came through thin, polite, and careful. The kind of tone people use when they want credit for being decent.

"I'm happy for you," she said, as if tolerance were a gift she'd wrapped just for me.

I wanted to believe she meant it, and maybe she did. But knowing what I'd experienced in the past with her, I couldn't help being cautious. Every word felt weighed, measured, sanitized for respectability. It wasn't kindness. It was distance disguised as civility.

When the call ended, I stood for a long moment staring at the silent phone, the winter light pouring through the kitchen window. I could already feel it starting; the slow unraveling that always came when he decided he wanted to "make things right."

It never really meant healing. It meant control, rearranged.

Then, another call from Dad.

"Your Uncle Mike wants to talk," he said, his voice casual, too casual, the way someone sounds when they're about to hand you a lit match.

That one made my stomach tighten. Uncle Mike had never been what you'd call open-minded. He was the eldest of the siblings, the one who carried their collective arrogance like a badge. He'd always spoken like his opinions were law, and disagreement was a moral failing.

"I don't think Uncle Mike is exactly LGBTQ-friendly," I said carefully.

My father didn't respond right away. Then, without warning, I heard the beeping tones of another line joining. He'd called him on the spot from his work desk phone and merged us into a three-way call.

I froze. I could hear papers shuffling, a faint exhale on the other end. Uncle Mike's surprise as he realized what was happening. Even he hadn't expected this ambush of a conversation.

"Hey," I said cautiously, adjusting my tone to sound neutral, already sensing the trap.

"Hey," he answered. His voice was even, too even. It was the kind of even that covers something sharper underneath.

"Your dad said you didn't think I would be okay with you marrying a man," he said. "I don't care about your choice. It's fine by me. You do you, man."

He said it fast, like he was trying to get through a speech someone had made him memorize. There was no warmth, no curiosity. Just the mechanical rhythm of someone fulfilling a social obligation.

Then, after a pause, he added, "I hope you have a nice life."

It wasn't what he said, rather it was how he said it. Final. Clean. Practiced.

A door closing politely in my face.

I could almost hear my father smiling on the other end, pleased with how neatly he'd wrapped the interaction. To him, it was proof that he'd brokered "peace." To me, it was confirmation that I'd just been publicly disowned, but with manners.

My father didn't seem to notice, or maybe he did and just didn't care. But I caught the intent instantly. I knew what have a nice life meant. It meant we're done here. It meant don't expect to be called again. It meant you're outside the circle now.

And honestly, I didn't care. I had zero respect for Uncle Mike or the kind of person he was; the kind who thinks civility can disguise cruelty. Whatever he thought of me was completely irrelevant. You reach a point where being tolerated feels more insulting than being rejected outright.

Two days before the party, my father called again.

He said Uncle Mike had been asking which route he should take to get to our house. His tone was clipped, like the logistics mattered more than the people involved.

I suggested two options. Both were simple, direct. My dad said Uncle Mike didn't like either. "He said he wasn't happy with those routes," my father added, as if it were meaningful, as if dissatisfaction with a map were a coded message I was supposed to decode.

I didn't have anything to say besides, "Those are the two I use." But I knew what it really meant. Uncle Mike was already backing out.

I wasn't surprised. I'd seen this performance before; the buildup, the half-promises, the sudden retreat wrapped in false politeness.

They'd done the same at Julia's wedding, leaving early in protest because of something printed in the program that didn't fit their expectations. I still remember Julia standing near the lake afterward, confused, hurt, trying to make sense of it, and telling me that they all seemed to have vanished.

When the day of the "after-party" arrived, I woke up already tired of it. The sky was gray and overcast, the kind of light that makes every color duller, flattening everything it touches. Even the coffee tasted muted. I moved through the morning like someone bracing for weather.

My dad showed up early with trays of food, the smell filling the house before I even saw him. Garlic, roasted meat, macaroni and cheese. Great smells, technically, but heavy, too, the kind that cling to the air and to your clothes. I could admit the food smelled good, but I couldn't shake the feeling that I'd been manipulated into hosting something I never wanted.

I told myself I'd just get through it. Smile. Play the part.

But I didn't set up tables or extra chairs ahead of time.

I knew better.

When he'd mentioned setting up earlier in the week, I'd told him, "They're easy enough to grab once people arrive." But the truth was, I already knew most wouldn't. I could feel it the way you feel a storm before it breaks—the pressure in the air, the stillness before the rain.

And I was right.

As the evening went on, only one uncle showed up. Four, maybe five cousins out of twenty trickled in, each one polite, friendly, careful. Their smiles had that strained politeness of people who weren't sure which version of the story they were supposed to believe. Everyone else stayed home. Maybe it was their way of protesting not being invited to the wedding, or maybe it was just easier to let silence do the work.

Either way, the empty driveway said everything. The cars that weren't there told the truth better than any words could.

My dad tried to play host, bustling around with plates and tongs, acting as if nothing was off. But I could see it; the disappointment tightening his jaw, the way his eyes flicked toward the door every time headlights passed outside and then away again when they didn't stop. He kept up the chatter, the performative charm, the forced laughter that never reached his eyes.

He had to have known. Maybe he'd believed they'd surprise him, that loyalty would win out, that blood would show up for him the way he demanded others to. But he'd overestimated them. And underestimated how well I knew them.

For me, it wasn't a loss. It was confirmation.

I was done.

The people who mattered had already shown up; for me, for Dan, for our life together. The ones who hadn't, I didn't need.

That night, after the last cousin left and the house went quiet, I walked through the living room and looked at the space where the extra chairs would have gone. There was nothing but open floor: clean, empty, peaceful. The hum of the refrigerator was the only sound. The air still smelled faintly of food, but even that was fading.

They'd stayed home thinking it would hurt me.

But it didn't.

It was a relief.

A quiet ending I hadn't realized I needed.

A final, wordless confirmation that I was right to stop reaching out.

I didn't block them. I didn't announce anything.

We just stopped talking.

And the silence that followed wasn't sad.

It was merciful.

It was the kind of silence that fills a room only after a storm has passed, when you can finally hear yourself think again, and realize the peace you've been chasing was just the absence of their noise.

If weddings reveal who shows up for you, funerals reveal who never left their performance behind. Both are stages, and in my family, every stage was another chance for him to rewrite the script. I used to wonder if he believed his own lines, or if he simply didn't care who noticed the contradictions. Either way, the performance always cost someone else their peace.

Author's Note: The Poison He Planted

There's something I need to admit.

While writing the previous chapter about the party after the wedding, I started to wonder if maybe it wasn't that bad. Maybe I was being overly sensitive. Maybe other people had it worse, with parents who hit and punch, parents who left, or parents who made their pain obvious instead of hiding it behind a smile and a phone call.

That thought slid in quietly, the way his voice always used to. The same voice that made me question what I saw, what I felt, what I remembered.

It whispered: You had a roof. You had food. You had it pretty easy.

For a while, I listened and unfortunately, I stopped writing this memoir.

And then I realized: that doubt was his doing.

It was one of the poisons he planted in me long ago; the kind that doesn't kill you, but grows quietly inside you until you start pulling your own truth apart.

He trained me to minimize pain, to distrust my own memory, to see control as care. That's what makes this kind of damage so hard to name. You grow up thinking survival was luck instead of labor.

But healing, I've learned, is the act of gardening the self—of finding every poisonous seed he buried in me and pulling it out, one by one.

Writing this book is part of that. Every chapter is another weed torn from the soil.

And if you've ever doubted your own pain, or if you've ever told yourself it "wasn't that bad," please know this:

It doesn't have to be catastrophic to be cruel.

It doesn't have to leave a bruise to leave a mark.

What my father did was real abuse: quiet, relentless, dressed as love.

And what I'm doing now, finally seeing it for what it was, is real too.

The pages that follow are my proof. What comes next is mine. My life, my love, and the family I built from everything he couldn't control or break.

Chapter 13 – The Calls That Changed Everything

There are calls that change your day, and calls that change your life.

We got both within the same year.

It was the spring after several years of finally cutting my father off—Christmas 2017 had been the last time I saw him, the last time I let him speak into my life. By then, the silence he left behind had started to feel like oxygen. The world was quieter, my thoughts clearer. Dan and I were still learning what peace sounded like, and how it wasn't empty at all, just calm.

The call came on an ordinary afternoon, the kind where nothing seems remarkable until it suddenly is. The sunlight slanted through the blinds, the TV murmured in the background, and then the phone buzzed across the coffee table. Our adoption caseworker's number lit up on the screen.

"Are you sitting down?" she asked, her voice carrying that half-laugh people use when they're about to say something life-changing.

We weren't.

"You've been chosen," she said. "A baby girl was born this morning. The birth mother has already signed the paperwork. You need take off work so you can pick her up tomorrow."

For a few seconds, the room went still. Neither of us spoke. Then everything broke loose at once; our hearts, our breath, our plans. Dan let out a sound that was half-laugh, half-sob, and I think I did too.

The next few hours became a blur of motion and disbelief: quick calls to our bosses, texts flying back and forth with family, a scramble for car seats, formula, and diapers. We ran through the aisles of Target like contestants on a game show, giddy and nervous and slightly terrified. Later that night, too wired to sleep, we hit a drive-through because neither of us had remembered dinner.

The house looked the same when we got home, but it wasn't. It had shifted somehow, like it knew something we didn't. Every corner seemed to hum with anticipation, as if it were already waiting for her to arrive.

The next morning, the highway stretched ahead of us to the west; a few hours of nerves and coffee and quiet disbelief. The sun rose at our backs, flooding the dashboard with light. Every few minutes, one of us would say it out loud, just to make it real: "We're parents."

When we reached the hospital, the nurses greeted us like they'd been expecting us all their lives. There was kindness in their smiles, the kind that comes from people who've seen both heartbreak and hope and still choose to root for the latter.

The birth mother had already been discharged, but the room still carried the soft trace of her—an open window letting in the faint scent of grass, a folded blanket on the chair, the ghost of lotion and antiseptic in the air. It was quiet but tender, as if the space itself understood what had just happened there.

The nurses showed us a short series of required videos dealing with safety, feeding, and car-seat instructions. They were awful in that bureaucratic, overcautious way only hospital training videos can be: grainy footage, bad acting, endless disclaimers. But we didn't care. We would've watched ten more if it meant getting to the part where we held her.

And then we did. They placed her in our arms, and for a moment the whole room seemed to exhale with us. She was impossibly small, a bundle wrapped in hospital cotton, yet she carried the weight of every hope we had been holding for years. We couldn't stop staring at her. Every twitch of her fingers, every soft sigh felt like proof that we were finally parents. One of the nurses snapped photos of us together; the first official family portraits, and even she couldn't help smiling at the way we clung to each other. Our social worker, standing in the corner, had tears in her eyes. She knew how much we wanted this moment, and how much this day had cost us in doubt and heartache. Now it had come. The day we wondered if it would ever arrive was here, and in our arms was our small bundle of joy.

Then, in an almost cinematic twist, one of the nurses appeared at the door, grinning. She told us there had been a drawing for a massive baby gift basket that included a year's worth of diapers and formula, and somehow, our new daughter had won.

We laughed through our disbelief, both of us stunned by the symmetry of it all. It felt like the universe was winking, reminding us that joy sometimes arrives with its own small miracle.

After the paperwork was signed with the social worker; final signatures, official congratulations, flashes of camera phones, the nurses and social worker left us alone in the room to get to know our daughter.

And that's when everything changed again.

Two nurses came in, faces tight, smiles practiced. You could tell right away that whatever they were about to say, they didn't want to.

"We're so sorry," one began, her voice steady but trembling at the edges. "But the hospital director has decided to reverse the decision."

For a few seconds, the words didn't register. We just stared at her, still holding the joy, still half-smiling, thinking maybe she meant the gift basket or a form that needed to be re-signed. Something simple. Something fixable.

But her words came again—slowly this time, careful and devastating.

"The director didn't feel comfortable releasing the prize into this family scenario."

This family scenario.

The phrase landed like a slap. It was the kind of wording that hides behind formality, the kind that sounds neutral but drips with bias.

The nurses shifted, embarrassed. One of them muttered under her breath, "She means a same-sex couple." The other added quietly, "We're furious, but we can't override it." Their eyes said everything their jobs wouldn't let them say.

For a moment, none of us moved. The air felt heavier, like the whole room had tilted. I could feel Dan's hand brush mine, steady but shaking. There wasn't anything to say. We'd already learned long ago that some battles are fought with silence.

And then something unexpected happened.

One nurse slipped out of the room, her jaw set. Moments later, another came in carrying a box. Then another. And another.

Each one said some variation of the same line:

"We're not permitted to give out unopened supplies."

And then—tear, crack, rip—they'd open a flap on a box of diapers, a quick tear of a pack of formula, then the top of a box of tiny onesies.

"Oops," they'd say, smiling through their frustration, "now it's opened, so it's yours."

It was subtle at first, a small rebellion disguised as routine. But soon it became a rhythm—rip, tear, smile. A quiet act of defiance against the kind of prejudice they couldn't confront directly. By the time they were done, the room looked like Christmas morning.

There were bottles, blankets, burp cloths, everything a newborn could need, half-opened, technically now ours and entirely full of kindness. The air felt lighter again, full of something sacred that prejudice couldn't erase.

We were overwhelmed. Not just by the generosity, but by the unspoken truth behind it: that goodness, real goodness, still existed in the cracks where hate tried to grow.

When the final signature was at last accepted and the social worker nodded, we carried our daughter out through the same doors that had tried to close on us.

The drive home was euphoric; sunlight flooding through the windshield, the soft sound of her breathing in the backseat, the radio humming quietly. Every mile felt like a small miracle. For the first time in years, joy felt unguarded.

Everyone came to meet her. Friends brought casseroles; family arrived with gifts; the house buzzed with laughter and baby powder. The air was full of warmth, of tiny clothes drying on racks, of bottles clinking in the sink. We barely slept, but exhaustion had never felt so good.

A week later, the phone rang again.

The tone in the caseworker's voice was enough.

I didn't even need her to finish the sentence to know what was coming. There's a way people talk when they have to break something fragile; it's careful, gentle, but still heavy enough to shatter you.

The birth parents had changed their minds.

They'd decided a relative would raise the baby instead.

The agency called it a disruption.

Such a tidy, clinical word for a kind of heartbreak that can't be measured.

The next morning, the drive to the adoption agency felt endless. The highway blurred, mile markers counting down to something neither of us wanted to face. It rained lightly, the kind of drizzle that smudges everything gray. We didn't talk much. What could we say? The car seat in the back felt like a wound we couldn't look at.

When we arrived, the staff ushered us into a small conference room, away from everyone else. There were tissues on the table, which felt cruelly prepared, like they already knew the choreography of our grief.

We'd brought the few things she loved; the soft onesie she'd worn home from the hospital, the small stuffed animal she always clutched, her favorite pacifier with the tiny chew marks on the side. The caseworker told us we could take as much time as we needed. She didn't have to say that "as much time" still meant "not enough."

We held her until she fell asleep. Her head rested perfectly in the space between our shoulders. We kissed her forehead and placed her back into the nearby basinet.

There's no way to prepare for the moment you have to give back a child who already feels like yours. You just move through it, mechanically, quietly, as if your body has gone on ahead while your heart stays behind.

Walking out felt like leaving a piece of ourselves in that small room. The sound of the door closing behind us was sharper than it should've been. The car ride home was silent; no music, no talking, just the rhythm of tires on wet pavement and the weight of absence sitting between us.

For days afterward, the house sounded wrong, too quiet, like the air itself was waiting for her return. The silence had edges. Nights were the hardest. We didn't hear her soft cries for formula or the rustle of blankets when she needed a quick change. But we couldn't sleep anyway, even though she wasn't here to wake us up. Every small sound, like a floorboard settling or the hum of the fridge, made us look up, half expecting to hear her.

We packed away the diapers, bottles, the blankets, and the closet shelves still lined with half-opened boxes from the nurses who had tried to make it right. The agency gently advised us to hide everything, to put it out of sight so we wouldn't torture ourselves by looking at it every day. So we did. We closed the closet door, stood there for a long moment, and let the quiet settle in around us.

It was the sound of something ending; soft, merciful, and unbearably still.

Months later, in 2020, our phone rang again.

This time, the baby wasn't born yet.

But that's a different kind of call—the kind that changes everything in the right direction.

We were sitting on the couch watching TV when Dan's phone rang. I was already halfway down the hallway toward the bathroom, calling over my shoulder, "If that's the social worker, tell her I know the medical forms expire in two days. We'll get them redone soon!" With COVID, we were trying to stay inside and pushing off even well-visit checks to limit our exposure in the beginning.

Dan stumbled with his phone and then was able to answer after a few rings.

I remember the sound of the TV fading behind me, the hum of the bathroom fan, the ordinary shape of that moment; seconds before everything changed again.

When I came back down the hall, Dan was still on the phone, but his face had shifted. He was standing now, pacing slightly, eyes wide with something between shock and awe. Then I heard him say, "Wait—what? Really? Are you serious?"

I didn't even need him to tell me. I knew.

We'd been chosen again.

This time, the call wasn't for a baby already born. It was from a birth mother who was still pregnant and had chosen us ahead of time. She was making an adoption plan early, carefully, intentionally. And for the first time, we had the chance to walk that path with her from the very beginning.

Because it was during COVID, we couldn't meet her in person, but we talked over Zoom, which was awkward at first, then easy. She was kind, soft-spoken, and thoughtful in a way that made every word feel considered. We didn't want to ask too many questions or get too hopeful, but something about her steadiness felt different. It didn't feel like a door opening suddenly; it felt like one being opened for us.

When her due date came and went, we got nervous. Then another day passed. And another. Still nothing. Every hour felt like its own small eternity, each morning starting with the same question: "Have you heard anything yet?" And the response, "I hope she didn't change her mind."

Then finally, on day ten, we got the call.

"She's here," the social worker said. "Your daughter's here."

Piper had decided to take her time entering the world.

We were told we could come the next day to pick her up.

The drive to this hospital felt both familiar and completely new—this time, cautious hope replacing fear. The roads were nearly empty, still under the strange hush of the pandemic. Every town we passed seemed paused mid-breath, storefronts dark, traffic lights blinking to no one.

When we arrived, we weren't even allowed inside. We pulled the car up to the front entrance, hearts pounding, windows down to hear every word. A nurse came out to collect our car seat and took it back into the hospital. Then we waited for another eight to ten minutes.

A nurse appeared, dressed head to toe in protective gear: mask, gloves, face shield, full gown. Even through all that fabric and plastic, I could tell she was smiling.

She carried Piper carefully, her arms holding the seat handle protectively, as if handing over the most delicate secret in the world.

"Congratulations," she said, her voice muffled but warm.

She opened the back door and placed her car seat into the holder until it snapped into place. We pulled away from the front and around the corner into the back of the parking lot. We made sure she was secured into the car seat—tiny hands, impossibly soft skin, eyes barely open—and just like that, she was ours.

We sat there for a moment, stunned, just watching her breathe. Then we drove off, the social worker waving from the same parking lot as we pulled away.

The ride home was quiet in the best way. Every few minutes, one of us would glance into the back seat, just to make sure she was still there, still real. The sun was low, the kind of gold that makes everything feel touched by grace.

"She's really here," one of us whispered. Then again, a few minutes later, just to be sure.

When we carried her through the front door, the house that had once been too quiet finally sounded right again. The air seemed lighter. Even the walls felt softer, as if the house itself exhaled.

After years of learning what peace sounded like, we finally heard it for real.

The days that followed blurred into something new; routine and miracle at once. Piper was amazing from the very start, her presence filling corners of the house I hadn't even realized were empty.

Dan shifted his career almost overnight, transforming the basement into a small classroom with a desk, a webcam, and the faint echo of his voice carrying up through the floorboards. By nine in the morning, he'd already finished teaching his students, coffee cup still warm beside him, while I sat upstairs feeding Piper. Then, like clockwork, he would climb the steps, workday behind him, and scoop her into his arms. From that moment on, the rest of the day belonged to her, and I started my workday from the home office. Our lives became a rhythm of handoffs and shared responsibility; quiet teamwork stitched together by love.

Most days we ate lunch together, the three of us gathered around the kitchen table as if it had been waiting all along to be complete. Piper's babbles and laughter turned the simplest meals into occasions. Sometimes, in the afternoons, I'd steal an extra break from work just to wheel her stroller into the driveway. I'd stand there, watching her legs kick and her eyes widen at every bird that fluttered overhead, every car that rolled by, every noise she seemed to discover as if it were treasure. The world had become new again because she was seeing it for the first time, and through her, so were we.

One summer afternoon, when her skin started reacting to the sunlight, we improvised by setting up a small inflatable pool inside the garage. One of the cars stayed parked outside for a week, leaving room for water and laughter. The smell of chlorine mixed with concrete, and dust, and somehow it felt like magic. Piper adored it. She sat in her bath basin and slapped her hands against the water, droplets flying across the garage, her grin so wide it seemed to brighten the walls themselves.

Evenings often ended with slow walks around the block, her stroller rolling steadily as the neighborhood drifted by in soft increments. Nothing about it was grand or extraordinary, yet every step felt weighty, sacred. These were the kinds of moments we had almost convinced ourselves might never happen, and now they were simply ours.

Then came the first milestone: the date on the calendar when the adoption could no longer be reversed. We didn't celebrate with champagne or balloons. Instead, we let the relief wash quietly over us, the way peace often arrives; without spectacle, just certainty. A line crossed, a promise kept. She was ours in a way that no one could ever undo.

Seven months later, another milestone arrived. The final court hearing. Because of COVID, it happened not in a solemn courtroom with polished wood and echoing footsteps, but right there in our living room. We set the iPad on the coffee table and dressed in nice clothes as if the occasion deserved nothing less. Piper sat between us, her tiny body nestled securely, as the judge smiled through the screen and our lawyer beamed with pride. A screenshot captured the moment, becoming the family photo we hadn't known we needed, with Dan's arm around me, Piper between us, and all of us smiling.

When the gavel came down, even virtually, it felt real. Official. Complete. Soon after, Piper's new birth certificate arrived in the mail, our names printed neatly where once there had been blanks.

We were a family; not just in our hearts, not just within the walls of our home, but in the eyes of the law, the state, and the world.

And for the first time, we didn't just feel like parents. We were, officially.

Chapter 14 – The Calls I Didn't Answer

I was working from my home office that morning, the familiar hum of routine anchoring me in place. Through the wall I could hear Dan moving around the house, his voice drifting in now and then as he spoke to Piper. She was curled on the family room rug, half-watching an educational show while scattering toys in an orbit only she seemed to understand. I asked him if he could keep things quiet for the next hour, and he said he'd take Piper down to the basement to watch TV, since it was farther from my office door.

It should have been a quiet morning. Ordinary. Predictable. Except for the strange voicemail from the night before.

The call hadn't even rung through. My phone is set to silence unknown numbers, so it had gone straight to voicemail. The message was unsettling in its vagueness: a doctor's voice, clipped and formal, but with no name given, no mention of which "dad" he was talking about. Just an urgent request to call a number back. The area code was local, but without names or details, I'd dismissed it as spam. After all, who leaves a message like that without identifying themselves?

But now, in the brightness of the next morning, unease settled heavy in my chest.

I didn't have long to dwell on it. I was minutes away from a live demo on camera—one of the most important I'd ever delivered. The bot I'd built for a customer had already saved them countless hours of manual work and an error rate of

0%, and today I was showcasing it to a virtual room full of executives, higher-ups, and decision-makers. This wasn't just a slide deck. This was live, running against their own network and systems on a laptop they sent to me. No edits. No script. No safety net.

The ring light glared against my eyes, throwing heat across my face as I tested the camera. The webcam framed every movement, every breath. I already hated public speaking, but public speaking while being broadcast into thirty tiny boxes of serious, watchful faces? That was torture. Every time I reached for my water, every scratch of my nose or shift in my chair felt amplified, as if the camera might be zooming in for everyone to see. And in twenty minutes, I was supposed to go live.

That's when my phone lit up again. Another silenced call.

This time, the voicemail left no room for dismissal.

The doctor said my name. He gave his name, and my father's. His tone was urgent, precise, the kind of voice doctors use when they don't have time to soften the blow. He said my father hadn't answered his phone. They couldn't reach him. Blood test results had come back. It was an emergency. "You need to get to the house quickly," he said. "Or call the police for a wellness check. Time is critical."

I just sat there staring at the screen. Fifteen minutes until my camera came on. My chest was already buzzing with nerves, and now this?

Is this really happening now?

And why me? Why am I the one getting this call? Why am I an emergency contact? Did he not get the hint after all these years? I hadn't listed him anywhere on my medical forms, legal paperwork, or work emergency contacts. I'd been careful about that. And yet here I was, pulled back in against my will.

My hands shook as I picked up the phone and called my sister. She lived sixteen hours away, but I had no one else to reach for in that moment. My voice was tight with panic and disbelief. "I just got a voicemail from a doctor about Dad," I told her. "They said it's an emergency. And I'm about to go on camera in fifteen minutes for a live demo. I can't do anything right this second."

She stayed calm in the way I couldn't. She asked for the doctor's name and number, promising she would call immediately. Then she looped in our brother, who lived closer to Dad's house, and asked him to check in person.

By the time I went live, the wheels were already in motion. I didn't know what was happening on their end, only that I had no choice but to steady my hands and focus.

And somehow, despite the storm in my chest, the presentation went flawlessly. I hit every mark. I demonstrated every feature. The bot ran and did all of the work in record time, without any errors. People nodded in their video windows, smiled, sent applause reactions in Microsoft Teams. Congratulatory chat messages scrolled by. I rocked it. And none of them had any idea that in the background, my father's life might have been unraveling.

When the camera went off and the meeting ended, I exhaled so hard it felt like I'd been holding my breath the entire hour. Then I called my sister back.

She filled me in quickly. My brother had gone to the house and found him. Dad had promised to go to the hospital, and somehow, he drove himself there. The diagnosis: a rare blood disease from a tick bite. Treatable. Curable, even.

But the details didn't add up. That day, somehow, Dad had Uncle Ray's phone, while Uncle Ray had his. How do you even mix up phones like that, unless your mind isn't fully present? And why, when everyone had been calling his cell over and over while the two of them were in the same house, didn't he hear it ringing from Uncle Ray's room in the old dining room?

I almost called him myself. I almost let my number flash across his caller ID, almost gave him the satisfaction of knowing I was worried, that I still cared enough to check. But I didn't. I held back. And even now, I'm glad I did. I hope that doesn't make me sound like a monster.

After everything, I didn't owe him that piece of me—not my voice, not my concern, not the proof that he could still pull me back into orbit.

I worried, even as I thought it, that someone might judge me for not calling back, for not rushing to his side. That maybe it made me sound heartless, or worse, like a monster. But the truth is, I wasn't the one who built this distance. He was. He wrote the rules years ago, and I learned them by surviving them.

An emergency contact is supposed to be the person you trust most, the person who will drop everything when the worst happens. I never had that in him. When things were hard for me as a kid, he didn't show up; he made them harder. He was the one turning life into an emergency, then disappearing into his bedroom with a drink or a nap while the rest of us scrambled to hold it together.

And yet somehow, decades later, he still scribbled my name down on a form and expected I'd come running. That's the cruel symmetry of it. He got to decide when he wanted me close, as if my childhood hadn't already proved that the closeness was always one-sided. He never earned the right to expect me in the room when things got tough. Not then. Not now.

So no, I didn't call. I didn't let my number light up his phone. Because with someone like him, even that tiny flicker of my name showing up on his caller ID would have been enough ammo. He would have twisted it into proof that he still had me wrapped around his finger, that no matter the years or the distance, I was still orbiting him.

I chose not to give him that. Not my voice, not my concern, not the satisfaction of believing he could still summon me in a moment of crisis.

And if that makes me sound like a monster, then maybe people don't understand what it costs to be raised by one.

Later, my brother told me he could see the hole in the ceiling over the family room from the driveway; king-sized, wide open to the sky, water damage spreading like veins through plaster. He shook his head and said, "That's probably how the tick got into the house."

And somehow, that detail stuck more than anything else. Of course a house like that—rotting, broken, unattended— would let sickness crawl in through the cracks. Just like the man inside it.

Many years after this memory, my youngest sister, Anna, and her mom came to visit us for the holidays and to meet Piper in person. I cooked dinner and we sat around the table together, a normal family gathering in every sense but one; the shadow of him was always hovering, waiting to be mentioned. At some point, I let myself wonder out loud: if Dad asked to meet for lunch, maybe I would consider it. Maybe, just maybe, I'd see what that conversation looked like.

Anna and her mom both shut it down instantly. "No. Bad idea. Don't do it." Her tone left no room for debate, and she didn't go into detail. But then she added something a few sentences later that cut deep: Dad had told her he was planning to write me out of his inheritance.

It was classic him. Control from a distance, punishment by rumor, dangling money like a chain he could still yank even after I had long since walked away. And if that wasn't enough, my brother told me Dad had been defending himself about the wedding and the phone calls prior, as if any of it were justifiable. He was still excusing the moment he asked us, "Who's the girl in the relationship?" as though our marriage was nothing more than a punchline for him to pick apart.

Every story, every comment, every rumor made it clearer: even in his decay, he was still reaching for ways to wound. And sitting at that table with my sister and her mom, hearing it all secondhand, I felt the same truth I had felt for years; there is no meeting in the middle with a man who lives to rewrite the script.

But part of me wondered what would happen if I did meet him. If I ignored Anna and Theresa's warnings and sat across the table one more time with my newly found power to stare right into his eyes and not back down. Would he apologize? Would he double down? Or would I finally see, up close, the man who had become nothing more than the rot in his own house?

I think about legacy often; not in terms of money, but in terms of patterns. My father's legacy isn't a list of assets or debts; it's the echo of control that shaped the way his children breathe. Cutting him off wasn't about losing a parent—it was about refusing to inherit his chaos. My true inheritance is the freedom to choose differently, to let my daughter grow up in a house where love isn't measured by obedience.

Chapter 15 – The Only Good Thing He Gave Me

In February 2023, my Aunt Kathy passed away. She was my dad's sister, and because she lived several states away, I only met her a handful of times growing up, maybe four or five in total. My sister Anna was the one who texted me with the news, which made me think Dad had asked her to.

I liked Aunt Kathy. First, she shared a name with my mom—spelled exactly the same. She was straightforward, the kind of person who said exactly what she thought without a filter. No games, no circling around what she really meant, just the truth as she saw it. I loved that about her. It was refreshing, especially in a family where so much was left unsaid or twisted into something else. She was cool, and in those few times I saw her, I always left wishing there had been more chances, or that she had lived closer. It says something that just a handful of interactions were enough to leave an imprint. In a family where words were so often weapons, her honesty felt like a rare kindness.

If Aunt Kathy didn't like what my dad said to me, or if she caught him trying to make a joke at my expense, she wouldn't hesitate. She would cross the room with a smile fixed on her face, and in that disarming way of hers, tell him exactly what she thought and why it was wrong. And somehow, he always seemed to respect her opinion. He would stop. He would leave me alone. She stood up for me in a way no one else dared to, and when he finally relented; agreeing with her, backing off, and walking away, she would turn back to me.

There was always that quick smile, that secret wink, before she rejoined the conversation she'd interrupted just to protect me.

I later heard that when she died, my dad's family rented a house in another state, close to where she used to live, and that the family flew in for the weekend to be together. They spent it laughing, drinking, posing for photos like the family was still intact. Everyone, that is, except me and Julia. We were the only ones not in attendance, from what I heard. It was as if we had been erased from the roll call, our absence treated as naturally as the weather.

I wish I could say I felt surprised, but I didn't. It was just confirmation of what I already knew; that sometimes the loudest part of being cut off is the silence. And the truth is, both Julia and I were happy not to be there. We didn't need to sit in a rented house and play along for pictures. We didn't need to drink or pretend or act like old wounds had never been inflicted. We stayed where we were, and in that choice, there was peace. We wouldn't have it any other way.

Later that year, in the fall, my Uncle Ray died. Anna broke that news to my brother and I in a group text and she specified that dad asked her to tell both of us. That loss cut deeper. He had always been my favorite uncle; the one who showed me kindness in small, steady ways that mattered most.

When I was a kid, spilling a drink in my father's house was practically a crime. It meant a disappointed voice or possibly a punishment that carried far beyond the spill itself. But with Uncle Ray, it was different. When my glass tipped over, he waved it off with a laugh: "Who cares? It's only a spilled drink." I was so upset I could barely get the words "I'm sorry" out, he tipped his own glass over on purpose, liquid splashing across the table in his kitchen. He grinned at me and said, "See? No big deal." Then he grabbed a dish towel, handed me another, and we wiped it up together, laughing. That moment carved itself into me; the first time an adult had shown me that mistakes didn't have to end in shame.

And I'll never forget Christmas Eve of 2017, where this book started and I changed my plans at the last minute to stop by my dad's house; a rare moment where I felt like I was the one controlling the script. Uncle Ray was there. We sat and talked for a few minutes; nothing dramatic, just a conversation. But it meant everything. He smiled. He talked when he hadn't been speaking much to anyone else around that time. That night was the last time I saw him, and I'll always carry the memory of those few minutes, knowing he chose to share them with me.

I'll always be grateful for what he gave me. He was the one who showed me my first steps around a computer, back when screens glowed black and white and DOS commands ruled the day. He made sense of things that seemed impossible. Later, when Windows 95 arrived, he sat with me again, making the confusing parts feel manageable and even fun. Those early lessons lit the path to the career I have now. That was a gift. That was him.

But even in his death, my father found a way to insert himself. Word reached me through a cousin, that Dad had told her to pass along a message: "Tell Jeff he better show up. He owes his career to Ray, after all. He introduced him to computers. And I expect him there in attendance to honor him."

As if grief was a debt to be collected.

The family wanted me to come to a rented cabin where they were planning some kind of "celebration of life," which, from what I later heard, was little more than a drunken weekend of yelling and chaos. If Uncle Ray had asked me, I would have gone. But he never would have asked. That wasn't him. He gave freely, without strings, without expecting a return. That was the difference.

No thanks. I didn't owe anyone my presence; not at the cabin, not at another stage play where grief was just an excuse to drink too much and scream at each other. I skipped it, and I have no regrets. They can all do them. I'm good.

That December, Julia and I got our annual holiday emails from Dad. His ritual. His version of "keeping in touch." Mine read, simply: Merry Christmas in the subject and then again in the message body. No warmth. No mention of my family. Just two words, like a formality he was checking off.

Julia's email, though, was different. Hers said: Merry Christmas, and I hope you and your family are doing well.

When we compared messages, I couldn't help but laugh a little, showing her my version. Just two words. She pulled out her phone and screenshotted hers to prove the difference. That was when her voice shifted from disbelief to fury. She hung up the call with me.

And then she called him, or maybe she left a voicemail, and told him flat out: "You're disgusting. You couldn't even wish

Jeff's family well? The only good thing you ever did in life was give me him as a brother." Then she hung up.

I hadn't expected her to say it, but when she did, I realized how much it mattered. For years I'd been the one holding the anger, carrying the silence, shouldering the absence. Hearing her say it out loud and to him, directly, was like a mirror. It was validation. It was love, too, the kind only a sibling can give.

By 2024, life was moving in a different direction altogether. We made the decision to leave Pennsylvania behind and move to Florida before Piper started school. After years of gray skies and cold winters, we wanted something different; something warmer, lighter, freer, and close to the ocean. Sunshine instead of snow shovels. Salt air instead of ice on the windshield. A chance to start fresh.

We found a beautiful spot not far from the beach, where we could ride e-bikes down shaded streets, take our golf cart to the pool, and live outdoors year-round. It felt like a reversal of everything we'd known. No longer bracing ourselves for the seasons, but opening the door to warmth and light almost every day.

While our dream home was being built, we rented a house nearby for seven months, learning how to breathe in this new rhythm of life. And then came the move. Our new home was larger than anything we'd ever lived in; high ceilings, wide glass doors that opened to the sky, rooms filled with light in a way that felt almost impossible at first. It wasn't just a house; it was a marker of survival, of arrival.

Luxury wasn't tons of windows or quartz counters or tall ceilings, though the house had those. Luxury was the feeling of being settled. Luxury was waking up and realizing the past didn't get a vote anymore. Luxury was knowing that we had built this life ourselves, brick by brick, decision by decision, far from the shadows that once swallowed us.

And the best part? We were only twenty minutes from Julia. For the first time in years, we could see each other often, not just through quick texts or rushed phone calls, but in the flesh. Sitting at the same table. Sharing meals at holidays. Taking walks on the beach in the winter with the sound of waves at our feet. Laughing without having to check the clock.

After everything, we were finally living close enough to make family feel like family again. That was the greatest gift; not the house, not the sun, not even the ocean, but the nearness of someone who truly knew me, someone who chose me back. And though we had left behind so many friends and family in Pennsylvania, we now had the space to welcome them here. Our home wasn't just ours—it was a place where people we loved could come, stay, and share in the sunshine with us. A kind of paradise with open doors and extra rooms, built not just for us, but for the life we wanted to share.

Chapter 16 – Breaking the Pattern

By 2025, life had begun to feel like something entirely new. After we moved into the new house, I finally felt the freedom to put words around everything I had carried for so long. The walls here were high and full of light, the air thick with possibility. For the first time in my life, I could breathe without waiting for the other shoe to drop.

That's when I wrote the letter—the one that appears at the beginning of this book in the epigraph. I typed it on my phone one afternoon, sitting in my new home office, letting the words pour out raw and unfiltered. I didn't plan it. I didn't workshop it. I didn't polish or second-guess. I just let the truth fall into place, line by line. When I stopped typing, I knew it was the truest thing I had ever written.

My husband read it first. He sat there quietly for a while, the blue glow of the phone lighting his face, before he looked up at me. His eyes softened, and his voice caught a little when he finally said it was powerful—extremely powerful. I could see in him the weight of what I had carried, and for once, I didn't feel alone in it.

Later, at dinner with my sister and her family, I slid the phone across the table and asked her to read it. She was quiet for a long time, her eyes moving steadily over the words. When she finally looked up, her voice was clear, steady, and full of conviction: it was one of the best things she had ever read. Then she handed the phone to my brother-in-law. He read in silence, too, then shook his head slowly as he passed it back; his only response a wordless acknowledgment, the kind that says, this is heavy, and it matters.

They both understood. They both felt it. My sister lived it, too. And for the first time, I realized this wasn't just my truth, it was a truth that could be seen, validated, and shared. My voice didn't echo back empty anymore. It landed.

Not long after that, I made another decision. I opened my phone, scrolled to my reminders, and deleted the one that popped up every year for my father's birthday. That tiny notification had haunted me long enough. Every time it appeared, it was like a hook pulling me backward, dragging me into a place I no longer wanted to live. I had no intention of calling or texting him. Why keep a reminder for something that no longer had a place in my life? Removing it felt like pulling out a weed; one of the poison seeds he had planted years ago.

When his birthday came, the notification didn't. But I still noticed the date. My brain still carried the reflex, like a muscle memory I hadn't trained out yet. Maybe one day that reflex will fade. Maybe, years from now, the day will come and go without any spark of recognition. That's the future I want: a day when the calendar is just a calendar again, stripped of his shadow.

A month later, I went one step further. I changed his contact to a silent ringtone and a silent text tone. That way, if he ever sent something beyond the usual once or twice-a-year messages, I would see it on my terms.

His typical messages of "Merry Christmas" or "Happy Birthday" were never warm anyway. They weren't connection; they were obligation typed out in a handful of words. A performance of civility. I don't respond anymore. I won't. Because even the smallest reply might feed the idea that he still had me wrapped around his finger, that I still lived in his orbit. And I'm done with that.

That summer, Dan, Piper, and I went to Cancun for a week. A chance to step away from unpacking, house projects, and the endless logistics of settling in. It just so happened that Father's Day fell while we were there. Father's Day in paradise.

We didn't go for the holiday; we went for the ocean, the sand, the chance to exhale, relax, and have fun. But being there when the day arrived gave it a strange kind of poetry.

Our little family of three spent that day together; me, Dan, and Piper. We swam in the ocean and pools that shimmered turquoise. We laughed until our faces ached. We let the sun press warmth into our shoulders, the kind of warmth that sinks deeper than skin. Messages buzzed in from loved ones wishing us a happy Father's Day, celebrating the family Dan and I had built together. And then, the next morning at breakfast, something hit me like a soft wave: not once the day before had I thought about my own father.

For the first time in my life, Father's Day came and went without his shadow stretching across it. I hadn't braced myself for a phone call, like in earlier years. I hadn't rehearsed conversations in my head, playing out the dance of lies and half-truths. I hadn't felt the weight of obligation pressing down. I simply lived the day; fully, freely, and joyfully.

And in that moment, I felt something like grace. Not the kind handed down from him, because there never was any, but the kind you stumble into after years of fighting for air. Forgetting him on Father's Day felt like paradise in itself. A breath of fresh, salt-sweet air. Proof that I was no longer tethered to the man who had once defined so much of my life.

That day, I remembered what freedom feels like; not in theory, not as a wish, but in practice. Freedom is silence where there used to be noise. Freedom is choosing who gets to matter in your life. Freedom is the absence of dread. Freedom is forgetting him, and remembering me.

The letter I wrote in the beginning of the year began as a private act; words stored quietly on my phone, never meant to be anything more than my own declaration of freedom. But looking back now, I realize it was the natural ending to a story that had been trying to write itself for decades.

It was never about him. It was never about changing his mind, or earning his approval, or rewriting the past so it would finally make sense. It was about me. About reclaiming the voice I had once swallowed. About refusing to live in the orbit of his silence and his demands. About finally naming what had always been true: I am free.

For years, I thought freedom would come the day he stopped calling, or the day I stopped caring. But it didn't. It came in moments—the first holiday without dread, the first birthday without obligation, the first Father's Day I forgot him completely. It came when my family stopped meaning the family I came from, and started meaning the family I chose and built.

That's why I wanted this book to begin with the letter— because everything else was leading here. To the day I could write the words I needed, and then live them.

And now, in the life I've built, I see proof every day that cycles can be broken. Our home is filled with laughter, softness, and safety—the very things I once thought were impossible at my father's house. Piper is growing up surrounded by the love I never knew as a child (from my father), and everyone who meets her tells us the same thing: she's amazing and we're doing a great job. That affirmation matters, but what matters more is knowing I am giving her what I once needed most. I may not know all the right ways to parent, but I know exactly what not to do. And sometimes, that's the truest inheritance I can offer her: a life free from the weight I carried.

And yet, even as I write these words of release, I know there is one more letter that waits—a letter not for him, but for me. A letter meant for the day he is finally gone, when silence will be permanent and the temptation might be to search for closure where there is none. That page belongs to the Afterword. But here, in this chapter, I leave him behind once more—and walk forward with my own.

Afterword: For Me, Not for Him

(To be read on the day my father dies)

You're gone now.

And I didn't come.

I didn't stand in a pew or sit in a folding chair.

I didn't listen to stories told by people who never saw the inside of what I lived through.

I didn't wear black and pretend that grief looks the same for everyone.

Because for me, this isn't grief.

It's relief.

It's quiet.

It's a closing door that no longer creaks open in the night.

No more holding my breath when the phone rings.

No more hearing your voice in my head, sometimes louder than my own.

I mourned my childhood while I was still in it.

I buried my trust when I barely knew what trust meant.

I held funerals in secret for the parts of me you shattered—

the joy that flinched, the laughter that hid,

the boy who never got to just be a boy.

You taught me silence, and I mistook it for strength.

You taught me fear, and I mistook it for normal.

You taught me to disappear in plain sight.

But now I see you for what you were.

Not a father.

Not a protector.

Just a man who chose control over connection—

who weaponized love like a knife behind his back.

This moment isn't yours.

It's mine.

It's the first moment I've ever had where you can't touch me—

not with guilt, not with shame, not with stories you rewrote to make yourself the victim.

I don't hate you anymore. Hate was just another leash, and I've taken that off too.

You were the storm I learned to stand in.

And though I won't thank you for it, I'll continue to walk forward dry.

The story ends here, not because I forgive you, but because I finally don't need to.

So no, I didn't come.

Because you taught me how to leave.

And now I finally have.

You Are Not Alone

When I finished writing this book, I thought about the people who would hold it in their hands. Maybe someone like me years ago—unsure if they'll ever feel free. If that's you, let me tell you something I wish I had heard sooner: you are not alone, and you don't have to carry it forever.

Thank you for letting me tell my story. Thank you for listening. If it stayed with you, talk about it. Share it, please. Because every time we speak the truth out loud, the silence loses a little more power.

And if this book resonated with you, the most powerful way you can help is by leaving a review. Reviews not only support authors, but they also help other readers find it.

If you or someone you know is experiencing emotional, psychological, or physical abuse, confidential support is available 24/7 through the National Domestic Violence Hotline at 1-800-799-SAFE (7233) or thehotline.org.

Reaching out for help is a sign of strength.